Praise for

WHITE AMERICAN YOUTH: MY DESCENT INTO AMERICA'S MOST VIOLENT HATE MOVEMENT—AND HOW I GOT OUT

"Christian Picciolini's *White American Youth* is a raw and honest memoir of his life as a leading activist and white power singer in the early American neo-Nazi skinhead movement. A cautionary tale about how even a smart kid from a stable home can get pulled into a world of violence and hate, it is as much a redemptive story of his journey out of that world and into a new life as co-founder of Life After Hate, an important anti-racist organization."

—MARK POTOK, former senior fellow, Southern Poverty Law Center

"Fascinating and timely... written with first-hand knowledge and authority... *White American Youth* not only tells Christian Picciolini's gripping story, but is filled with rare insights that put today's rise of white nationalism in perspective."

—ALI SOUFAN, former FBI special agent, *New York Times* bestselling author of *The Black Banners*

"Christian's journey exemplifies how hate and violence are unsustainable, and tolerance, forgiveness, and love are the only way forward. If Christian can change, there is hope for all humankind—a compelling and extraordinary story."

—JANE ROSENTHAL, co-founder, Tribeca Film Festival

"*White American Youth* takes the reader into the depths of the hate movement and sheds a valuable light on the mind-set of those who can be lured into this dark world. Christian's astonishing change of heart is a testament to our endless capacity for personal transformation."

—LONNIE NASATIR, regional director, Anti-Defamation League

"*White American Youth* is a very hard book to put down. Though the tale often takes the reader into disturbing territory, the storyteller's voice is filled with a beautiful, unwavering honesty. There have been countless sociological texts and documentaries devoted to the exploration of American neo-Nazi skinhead culture, but this book starts at the very beginning. Christian Picciolini was one of the first foot soldiers (and eventual leaders) of that movement, and though he has long since renounced those racist beliefs, there is a riveting emotional immediacy to his depiction of the process and mind-set that led him down the white power path. The issues and events dominating today's headlines are reminders that the roots *White American Youth* exposes are eminently germane. This memoir is not, however, merely a one-of-a-kind historical account. It is, first and foremost, the story of a human being who looks back on his earlier self with shock and horror, but it is told from the vantage point of one who refused to let his past define him. Though he will be forever haunted by deeds he cannot change, he lives with the joy of one who now understands the preciousness of every life—including his own."

—DON DE GRAZIA, author of *American Skin*

"Like a skinhead *Goodfellas*, *White American Youth* takes us along on a young man's journey to the dark heart of a distasteful organization, somehow making the narrator's descent every bit as understandable and compelling—and all the more tragic. It's a powerful and moving memoir that brought tears to my eyes."

—GERALD BRENNAN, author of *Resistance*, *Zero Phase*, and *Public Loneliness*

"*White American Youth* is a coming-of-age story about a relatively average all-American kid who finds himself at the center of organized hate. Christian Picciolini's memoir underscores how the search for universal needs such as identity, excitement, and belonging can influence adolescents to embrace extremism. Maybe most important, Picciolini's transformation from hatemonger to compassion advocate is an essential reminder of the human capacity for change and redemption."

—PETE SIMI, author of *American Swastika*

"If it's disturbingly easy to embrace the white power ideology, it's not as easy to leave behind. Christian's experiences in *White American Youth* will shock you, but it's his escape and transformation that will inspire. His honest, often brutal memoir charts a journey from hopelessness to redemption. A profoundly important book, and a riveting read."

—JOHN HORGAN, author of *The Psychology of Terrorism*

WHITE AMERICAN YOUTH

WHITE AMERICAN YOUTH

MY DESCENT INTO AMERICA'S MOST VIOLENT HATE MOVEMENT—AND HOW I GOT OUT

CHRISTIAN PICCIOLINI

hachette BOOKS

NEW YORK BOSTON

Hachette Books
Hachette Book Group
1290 Avenue of the Americas, New York, NY 10104
hachettebooks.com
twitter.com/hachettebooks

Originally published as *Romantic Violence: Memoirs of an American Skinhead* in May of 2015.

First Edition of *White American Youth*: December 2017

Hachette Books is a division of Hachette Book Group, Inc.
The Hachette Books name and logo are trademarks of Hachette Book Group, Inc.

The publisher is not responsible for websites (or their content) that are not owned by the publisher.
The Hachette Speakers Bureau provides a wide range of authors for speaking events. To find out more, go to www.hachettespeakersbureau.com or call (866) 376-6591.

Many names have been changed, including all participants in the hate movements who have not already been identified publicly in this regard.

Photography (author headshot) by Dennis Sevilla

Interior Photography (chapter photos) by Various

Publisher's Cataloging-in-Publication data

White American Youth / Christian Picciolini.
p. cm.
ISBNs 978-0-316-52290-8 (trade paperback), 978-0-316-52291-5 (ebook)
1. Picciolini, Christian. 2. Skinheads—United States—Biography. 3. Neo-Nazis—United States—Biography. 4. White supremacy movements—United States. 5. Ex-gang members—United States. I. Title.
HV6439.U5 P53 2015
320.5/6—dc23 2015900837

Printed in the U.S.A.

LSC-C

10 9 8 7 6 5 4 3 2 1

To my Buddy, my boys, and my Britton

Any intelligent fool can make things bigger, more complex, and more violent. It takes a touch of genius—and a lot of courage—to move in the opposite direction.

—E. F. Schumacher, *Small Is Beautiful*

CONTENTS

CONTENTS

FOREWORD

THE UNIVERSAL STRUGGLE FOR IDENTITY and belonging is what binds all of us together. It is this search, ultimately, that makes us human; that makes us, especially as children, vulnerable.

In the 1970s, when I was in the Runaways, the first all-female American rock band ever, I experienced all types of prejudice and bigotry as a woman. Sometimes it was all I could do not to give up altogether. But my guitar, along with my pen and my voice, led me out of that hollow fear and into a long and successful rock-and-roll career—one that, thankfully, I am still riding the powerful wave of today.

Thanks in large part to Kenny Laguna, my producer, manager, close friend, and lifetime confidant, I have arrived at this level of commercial success and have been able to carve out a life in music. Kenny was then and still is very much a mentor to me. Without his direction and aid, I would not be where I am today. He believed in me when most others didn't.

I met Christian Picciolini in 1996 while on tour in Chicago. I did not know about Christian then what I know now. We needed an opener, and when I saw his punk band, Random55, warming up on stage, I saw something special in their style and knew from some place deep inside

Christian Picciolini and Joan Jett, 1996

that they were the right ones. I approached Christian, who seemed low and withdrawn, backstage after the set. He seemed sad for some reason, and I talked with him for a little while, throwing my arm around his shoulder, trying to assuage his fears. I sensed that Christian had been like me as a struggling teenager, in a dark place, searching for identity and belonging—acceptance. He needed someone to believe in him.

Random55 ended up going out with us on the road that year, becoming our opening act for a string of shows. Christian and I had many more meaningful conversations, and I like to think that some of what I had to say helped him cope with whatever he was going through. I will always recall his dedication to music and his drive. I could tell that, at that time, he was seeking something from life, from his soul. Now he has written this incredible memoir, detailing and forcing out the truth, after all these years. And in doing so, he has, I hope, released his inner demons for good.

Compassion is an important human quality, and we all have the ability to tap into it. I have it for Christian's former, younger, troubled self. He was not a bad kid, but a kid trying desperately to belong to a community; to do something that mattered; to understand his loneliness and sense of rejection and abandonment. Hating the LGBTQ community, non-white minorities, Jews, and others when he was involved with the white-power skinhead movement is tantamount to a disgusting and immoral blind allegiance to hatred. And yet, Christian managed to do the one great thing that anyone who has ever been in his position—or is in his position today—could do: he learned to recognize his blindness, to see how violently corrupted he'd become. He was able to pick his head up from the muck of that ideology and see the error of his ways, to steer the ship in the other direction, and to get out. He not only left and at last denounced the movement in the late nineties, he went on to become a powerful voice against hatred, co-founding the nonprofit Life After Hate in 2009 and launching North America's first extremist intervention program.

White American Youth is Christian's testament to how frighteningly easy it can be to find yourself down the wrong rabbit hole with no way out. It is his tale of the only kind of redemption he will ever know. I admire him greatly, not because he once hated, but because he once hated and he fought hard against his own muddled determination and discovered that his prejudice and bigotry were paper-thin lies. We all have to discover life on our own path, find our truth. Christian writes his book to expose his truth, and we can be grateful in at least some small part for his courage in confessing how he ran on the dark side and what it is like to find yourself there and then breathlessly sprint for the light at the end of the tunnel. The result is a cautionary tale that furthers and educates us all.

In the end, we all need guidance, direction, and help along the road of life. We all need a mentor. For many, music is a major influence, and that can be used for good or bad. I was able to find myself through music, and, in a way, so did Christian. That night after the gig, throwing my arm around his shoulder was my way of showing empathy, compassion. Telling him that whatever he was feeling, I, like so many others, had been there too. Taking his band on tour was my handing of trust over to him. Like Kenny with me, I hope I was able to lead him, if only for a moment, out of the deep fog hovering around him. Christian pursued music in other capacities after that tour, and he maintained contact with Kenny and me through the years. I am so incredibly proud of his life's work since he left the white-power movement in 1995, and I can see the real change and transformation he has made.

So, if you want to practice empathy—or if you just want to experience one hell of a redemption story—come along for the ride and find out how it all started, where it went, and why it ended. Take the journey with Christian, and let yourself fall down alongside him. Feel the despair, violence, and rage as a young, impressionable boy climbs the rungs of the violent American white supremacist movement. Feel his fear and depression as he finally exits. Feel his sadness and hollowness after the battering waves of shame and isolation have at last ceased. And, beautifully, watch him change and grow, evolving into a fine human being who accepts *all* people, including himself.

Watch him turn into the man he always, deep down inside, wanted to be. Watch him make you proud to be a part of his experience, a part of this diverse global community, a part of this world.

Watch yourself change along with him.

Joan Jett

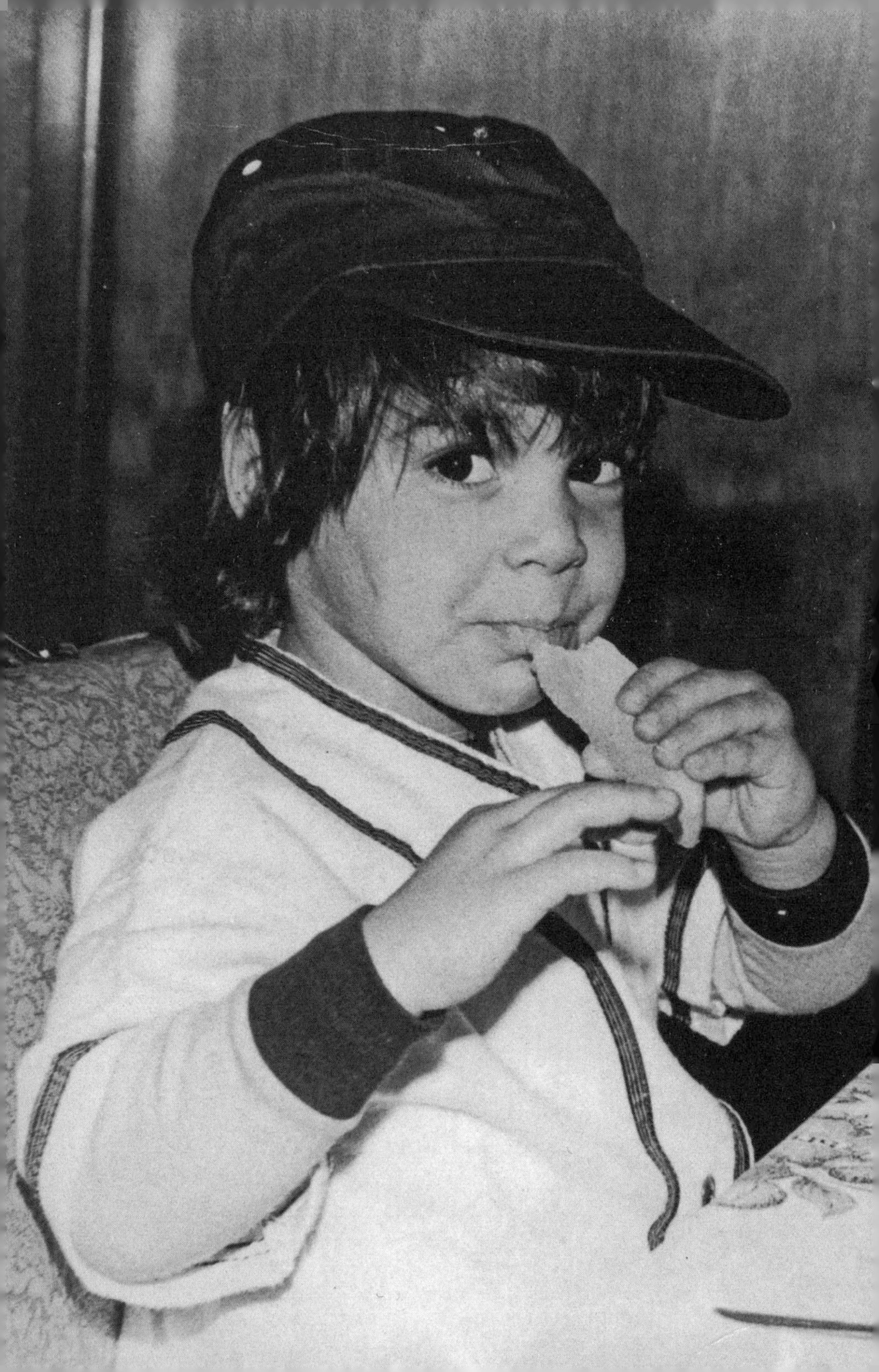

INTRODUCTION

CHARLOTTESVILLE. PORTLAND. NEW YORK CITY. Charleston. Oak Creek. Atlanta. Overland Park. Los Angeles. Denver. Las Vegas. Oklahoma City. Chicago. Washington, D.C.

Most people claiming any one of these fine American cities as their hometown will boast of their charming countryside, rolling landscapes, or bustling metropolitan abodes. But what they typically fail to acknowledge—what they may not even know themselves—is that in recent decades these cities and countless others across the United States have also been the sites of horrific, modern-day white supremacist terror attacks and killings.

Perhaps we've all heard of the few examples of these tragedies that received the proper contempt in the media: the horror in Oklahoma City in 1995 unleashed by white supremacist Timothy McVeigh, who, in a devastating act of domestic terrorism, bombed a federal building, killing 168 innocent civilians; the mass murder of nine African American churchgoers in 2015 within the sacred walls of Charleston, South Carolina's historic Mother Emanuel Church; the "alt-right" rally in Charlottesville, Virginia, in the summer of 2017, attended by hundreds of torch-wielding, clean-cut, young white men in pressed khakis and polo shirts who marched

Christian Picciolini, 1976 (Photo by Maddalena Spinelli)

and chanted, "The Jews will not replace us," a promise that one extremist attempted to follow through on when he sped his muscle car into a group of unwary counter-protesters, killing a brave female activist and ending her promising future. But aside from these three infamous events, most of the other hundreds, if not thousands, of yearly episodes of contemporary American hate-based violence and terrorism (the kind of racist brutality that, as I must always continue to confront, I might have enthusiastically participated in as a teenager) go underreported in or utterly ignored by our news media. As a result, so many Americans whose lives never took the dark turn into hatred that mine did and who didn't grow up minorities themselves, often finding themselves in the crosshairs of our nation's extremists, fail to realize the scope of our homegrown terrorism epidemic, fail to see the blood on all of our hands.

Whether we acknowledge it or not, the terrorists are always out there, promoting their propaganda, radicalizing our fellow citizens. Almost every week I receive an email or phone call from a frightened parent or friend asking me to help a loved one who they believe is on a course to becoming the next Charleston Shooter or Oklahoma City Bomber. Sometimes I'm able to connect with and help these troubled people—they know I once wore the shoes they walk in, and they see that there are paths away from the fate of guilt, toxic shame, and violence they hurtle toward. Still, I never forget that the odds of righting the course can be long, that any of these worried bystanders who contact me could be dead right, and I might watch helplessly as the troubled youth with whom I'd shared coffee and conversation with weeks before inflicts the next tragedy on our nation.

Many terrorism researchers and extremism experts agree that since the United States was attacked by al-Qaeda terrorists on September 11, 2001, more people have been killed on American soil by homegrown white supremacists than by any other extremist or terror group, both foreign *and* domestic combined.[1] Plain and simple, it's abundantly clear that America has a domestic terrorism problem. Yet, we—politicians, law enforcement, government, media, and many of our own citizens—fail time and time again to acknowledge it, to call it by its name. While we can be certain that we also have a terror threat in the form of aggrieved ideological actors from foreign lands, we must, if we have any hope of addressing it, understand that the biggest threat to American national security, democracy, and liberty has already been living and growing within our own borders for nearly 250 years.

Not all hope is lost. Based on my experience as a onetime white supremacist and my interactions with hundreds of others, both current and former, radicalization to violent extremism does not initially stem from ideology. Rather, I believe, many paths toward radicalization emerge from an individual's fundamental human search for identity, community, and a sense of individual purpose going wrong—and those paths are primed by a host of factors, including an individual's background, inclination toward violence, and sometimes their mental health. If during our journey to discover our essential human needs, we develop a distorted view of our path or stumble along the way into enough "potholes"—setbacks that often appear in the form of trauma, marginalization, or abandonment, untreated or undiagnosed mental health conditions, addiction, chronic unemployment, poverty, isolation, extreme neglect, or even extreme privilege—it is increasingly possible that without the proper triage and support systems in place, an otherwise positive life path can become one of inflicting suffering. Behind the "white nationalist" propaganda materials that have been found posted around college campuses across the country, hate-filled epithets seen scrawled on commuter trains, buses, and

---

[1] Shane, Scott. "Homegrown Extremists Tied to Deadlier Toll Than Jihadists in U.S. Since 9/11." *The New York Times*, June 24, 2015. Accessed September 9, 2017.

places of worship in our own backyards, and the conspiracy theories pitting one against the "other" that live and grow pervasively throughout the web and social media, there are opportunists with sinister agendas and a lust for manipulation waiting gleefully to fulfill those needs with empty promises of "paradise."

The allure of power, identity, and purpose is inherent in extremist cultures. I don't imagine there is much difference between why someone adopts a violent white-supremacist ideology and decides to slaughter a church full of black worshippers and why someone born in America's heartland flies to Syria to join an Islamist terror cell and bombs a crowded train station. Neither was born a terrorist, but somehow terrorism found them, and they found that it fulfilled them—or they somehow believed that it would. The violence is a vehicle, the ideology what they mistake for their license, to brutally project their own anger, pain, and self-hatred onto the innocent people they confuse as the sources of their woes.

If my experience as a boy who lost his way and became a white-power terrorist leader is anything to judge by, I am certain there has been at least one moment in these terrorists' lives in which the compassion of someone near them has opened their eyes, if only for a moment, and they have thought "What if I'm wrong?" and wondered if it was too late to get out.

Please listen when I tell you, it is never too late.

I write this book with optimism that my cautionary tale will help others to search for identity, belonging, and purpose in healthy, inclusive communities and will have the strength to walk away from empty promises, and that people will listen to those who encourage them to be compassionate human beings instead of finding a place among those who prey on the insecure and exploit their loneliness, fear, confusion, and feelings of worthlessness.

I hope that by exposing racism, hate will have fewer places to hide.

PROLOGUE

"Heil Hitler!"

Spotlights dare to glare through what was once a sacred house of prayer. We were in Weimar, what had recently become "former East Germany" after the wall had come down three years before.

Dense stage-fog snaked skyward around me. Like a new dawn rising, I had hoped.

"Heil Hitler!" I screamed again into the microphone.

Swirling around, feet swinging free in midair, I raised my clenched fist to my band. To the audience it was an amorphous signal of defiance. To my band, it was our cue to begin the next song. Veins were popping on my tattooed arms, sweat gleaming under the lights.

The band burst out with the force of a stampeding bull breaking free of its restraints. Music shattering any ancient echoes of holy hymns that had ever harmonized in this stone sanctuary.

I was eighteen years old and on a mission to save the white race. My voice filled the room.

We're White! Strong and free!
White supremacy!
White! We preach the truth!
White American Youth!

I'd ventured onto the path that led me to this stage four years before, not long after I was first introduced to the white-power skinhead band Skrewdriver and, oblivious to the ideologies it promoted, I fell in love with their music.

Then I met Clark Martell, a notorious white supremacist who terrorized Chicago, and I was oblivious no more.

It was early one evening just before the start of my freshman year of high school, and my friend Dane Scully and I stood zoning out, high on weed, staring at a squawking ebony crow perched atop one of the twisted light posts that lined the dead-end alley around the corner from Union Street and Division. We passed a joint back and forth, giggling like little girls.

The garages on either side of the narrow alley were crammed with a myriad of old furniture, stacked boxes of orphaned Mason jar lids, piles of plastic nativity sets, and unraveling lawn chairs. With no space left inside for even half a Fiat to squeeze in, we weren't worried about anybody pulling up on us. As far as we were concerned, these deserted backstreets existed solely as a gathering place for us kids—and chatty, odd blackbirds.

"Hey, Scully," I said, face pointed to the sky as I studied the winged intruder looking down on us from atop the flickering streetlight. "Do you think that old crow knows what we're doing?"

He laughed. "I don't know, man. But that's a seriously dumb question."

As Scully craned his neck to look up at the watchful bird, the shotgun roar of a car bursting up the alley broke the calm.

"Shit!" He tossed the joint.

I retrieved it. "Chill out, man. It's only Carmine." But as it turned out, I was wrong.

Carmine Paterno's primer-black 1969 Pontiac Firebird screeched to a skidding halt in the gravel beside us. I gawked at the stark contrast of the white death's-head skull freshly spray-painted on the corner of the matte hood. *Damn.* Could anyone be cooler than Carmine?

With the streetlamp flickering an amber glow on the car from above, the passenger door snapped open, and this older dude with a shaved head and black combat boots marched straight toward us. He wasn't unnaturally tall or imposing physically, but his closely cropped hair and shiny boots smacked of authority. Over a crisp white T-shirt, thin scarlet suspenders held up his bleach-spotted jeans.

He stepped across the beam of headlights and swiftly closed the distance between us. You'd have thought he'd turned in that alley specifically to hunt us down. I pulled back, wondering what the hell we'd done to piss this guy off.

Inches from me, he stopped and leaned in close, his beady, ashen eyes holding mine. The whites surrounding his granite pupils looked timeworn, intense. Barely opening his mouth, he spoke softly, with a listen-closely-now attitude. "Don't you know that's *exactly* what the Communists and Jews want you to do, so they can keep you docile?"

Not knowing exactly what the hell a Communist or a Jew was, or even what "docile" meant, my nervous instinct was to take a swift draw from the joint and involuntarily cough smoke straight into his face.

With stunning, ninja-like speed, this guy with the penetrating gray eyes smacked the back of my head with one hand and simultaneously snatched the joint from my lips with the other, crushing it with his shiny black boot.

I was speechless, frozen. I turned to Scully, but he'd vanished.

Blood retreated like flowing ice water through my veins and pooled in my heavy, tingling extremities. Shaking my head to regain my composure, I mustered enough confidence and tried to save face in front of Carmine. "What . . . what do you know . . . and who the hell are you, anyway? You're not my father," I sputtered. My voice sounded weak in my ears.

The stubbly, sharp-jawed man straightened up and gripped my shoulder firmly, drawing me in toward him. "What's your name, son?" His voice was steady and earnest.

I stammered. "Christian... Chris... Picciolini." "That's a fine Italian name," he said, his voice suddenly sounding kind. I braced myself for the inevitable knockout punchline my last name usually lent itself to. Sensing my nervousness, he leaned in and said, "Your ancestors were quite exquisite warriors. Leaders of men. You should be proud of your name." From my experience living in Oak Forest, I wasn't, though. "Did you know the Roman army, the Centurion commanders specifically, are considered among the greatest white European warriors in the history of mankind?" I didn't. He took out a folded piece of paper and a pen from his jeans pocket and scribbled the word "Centurion" on it. "And Roman women are divine goddesses," he added with a sly smile. That much I knew. I cracked a slight grin as he thrust the paper into my hand. "Go to the library and look it up. Then come find me and tell me what you've learned about yourself and your glorious people."

In the background, Carmine was leaning against his rumbling Firebird, glossed boots with white straight-laces covering his crossed ankles. He looked different. Focused. Pinching his cigarette and exhaling a thick, steely plume of smoke, he could have been James Dean. "The kid's cool, Clark. They're waiting for us. We should go."

"Well, Christian Picciolini," he said, firmly grasping my clammy hand, "I'm Clark Martell, and I'm going to save your fucking life."

With that, he nodded to Carmine, who jumped into his car and pulled it up alongside us. As quickly as he'd arrived, this guy climbed back inside the roaring beast, and he and Carmine tore off down the alley like a burning phoenix, leaving me surrounded by a cloud of exhaust.

1

GOLIATH

JAKE REILLY WAS LOOKING FOR a hapless soul that soggy April afternoon to be the target of his playground taunts, insulting kids for anything he could think of. He was the quintessential class bully—we called him "Goliath" behind his back—and he took great pleasure in routinely tormenting his less imposing eighth grade classmates at St. Damian Elementary School.

Today, for what seemed the millionth time, he chose me.

"Fuck you!" I fired off in response. I instantly wished I could take back my words as I spun around straight into the puffed-out chest of the grinning Goliath, who I realized had just rifled a handful of frozen grapes at the back of my head.

Fuck me.

The whispering chatterboxes wearing pigtails and plaid smocks and the skinned-knee jungle-gym rats who were in various puddle-like clusters on the playground wasted no time sensing the fresh blood in the water. Like hungry sharks, they closed in around us in a flash.

"Oh, look, isn't *Pick-my-weenie* tough?" Jake snickered while jabbing me hard in the chest with his chubby index finger. He loved to mangle my foreign last name and never ran out of creative ways to do it. How

Christian Picciolini, St. Damian eighth grade yearbook photo, 1987

I longed for a normal name like Eddie Peterson or Dan Cook or Jimmy Mayfair. Anything but the impossible-to-say Christian Picciolini—pronounced *Peach-o-lee-nee*—which made for all kinds of god-awful rhyming nicknames. *Pick-my-weenie. Suck-my-weenie. Lick-my-weenie.* Basically, anything-*weenie*. "You gonna tell your greasy Blue Island *dago* friends on me?" I grew up in Blue Island, a largely Italian neighborhood just outside of Chicago, where my parents had initially moved us to before landing in this suburban hellhole of Oak Forest, Illinois. "After school, cheese dick, I'm kicking your slimy *Eye*-talian ass back to the ghetto where you belong."

Jake didn't flinch at calling another student an "ass face" or a "dick with ears" whenever he felt like it. And he never lied about delivering a beating. But no one had ever dared challenge him with a "fuck you" before. Even though it had escaped my mouth by regrettable accident, I was a dead man, and everyone knew it.

"And if you don't show up again this time, pussy," he sneered, reeling me in close by my hood strings, "I'll fucking *kill* you."

Throughout eight years of elementary school I'd managed to invent enough excuses to avoid getting physically rearranged by Jake. But before I could muster a lie good enough to squeeze myself out of this particular jam, word spread faster than Nutella on toast. By the time the final recess bell rang, everybody knew about the fight. Except for the adults, of course. They were never there when you needed them.

I prayed one of the teachers—or the principal herself—would catch wind of the fight and put an end to it, but my prayers went unanswered. Doom loomed over me. Jake Reilly was much bigger—thick and tall and strong—and he'd surely have his cronies behind him. I'd be in it alone. I didn't have any friends in Oak Forest, or even Blue Island for that matter, to back me up. Other than the few ridiculous moves I had picked up when I watched Rocky beat up Mr. T in the movies or when I saw Rowdy

Roddy Piper smash Hulk Hogan over the head with a steel chair on TV wrestling, I had no clue how to fight or defend myself. But I couldn't back down now. Not this time. Not with four years of Goliath-dominated high school and an endless supply of ridicule on the horizon. Running away and being forever branded a "pussy" would be infinitely worse than getting pummeled.

Hoping that a long walk home would give me the time I needed to come up with a believable last-minute excuse to skip out on the fight, I took the scenic route after the final class bell rang. No such luck. All I could think about was how to convince my parents to let me transfer schools by tomorrow. But when I got there, my parents weren't home.

I changed out of my school uniform and navy slacks, grabbed my Santa Cruz skateboard, and apprehensively rode the six blocks to the park where the fight was to happen. I knew the entire eighth grade class would be there to witness my slaughter. People had even placed bets, I'd learned that afternoon, and for some reason proclaimed the loser—whom everybody fully expected to be me—would have to pay the winner ten bucks.

The moment this fight was over, I'd be ruined forever. Beaten. Stigmatized and forgotten. Cast atop the growing heap of junior-high nobodies who'd already been humiliated by Goliath. I couldn't care less about where I'd get the money to pay off the stupid bet; I could easily swipe that from my grandmother's purse without her knowledge. But I also knew that once I was dispatched into nothingness, there was no coming back. No one ever recovered from that.

As I rode up, I spied the giant lumbering confidently among the large group that had gathered like buzzards. Attempting to steady my shaking knees, I stepped off my board and struggled to take in my final gulps of air. Wiping away the nervous sweat that was already trickling down my brow, I thought one last time about running away. Maybe being exiled from the ranks of St. Damian's lower order wouldn't be worse than getting my face pounded by this massive beast.

As I retreated a step, planting my foot back onto my skateboard deck and turning to push off with my unsteady leg, some of the more spiteful onlookers suddenly broke into a clamor: "Pick-my-weenie! Pick-my-weenie! Pick-my-weenie!" Sensing my dread, the whole crowd turned against me.

I felt myself becoming dizzy and detaching from reality—fading into the ether—as I inhaled another series of quick, shallow breaths to try to calm my nerves. I turned toward my tormentor to accept my fate, just as a colossal wad of spit flew through the air and landed with a wet, gooey *thwack* dead on my cheek.

Hushed silence. Except for Jake, whose loud, guttural snort only meant that another loogie was imminent.

Anxious panic flushed through me, and before I could wipe his spit from my face, another glob of thick yellow phlegm struck me in the chest like a sniper's bullet and slowly dribbled down my turquoise Ocean Pacific T-shirt.

"What's wrong, dick breath?" Jake jeered, arms crossed over his chest. "Are ya chicken? *Bawk, bawk.*" The crowd formed a wall around us. "Suck-my-weenie ain't got no balls," he proclaimed. A shock of laughter broke out from the enclosing group of spectators.

Jesus Christ. This kid was *big*. Goliath was growing twice as big as he stood before me, while I shrunk smaller and smaller. This is suicide, I thought. He took a step toward me and spat a third time at the ground near my feet as if to mark the spot of my execution.

As the grip of the taunting mob tightened around us and we circled each other, the requisite trash talk began spewing from the ogre's crooked smile. Jake was name-calling. I was stalling. My swollen, purple eye from last week—the one I'd gotten when three black kids from

Blue Island jumped me and stole my bike—was finally beginning to heal, and I didn't want to have to explain a fresh one to my parents. Terror overtook me, and I could barely hear the crowd's increasingly muffled chants over my own fearful thoughts and the dull, echoing crackle of crisp leaves under my feet. "Quit being a faggot, like your pussy hairdresser dad, and stand still so I can friggin' kill you!" Jake made a beeline toward me.

The tendons in my arms tightened. I could feel my pulse dancing faster. It was the first time I remember feeling that I truly hated someone so much that I wished they were dead. My mind spun, trying to make sense of the emotions. My heart thumped out of my chest. Out of sheer despair, I summoned the nerve to step in with him and throw the first punch. Kill or be killed. What more could I lose? At least I'd go to my death valiantly. My baby brother, Buddy, would be proud that I wasn't a complete coward. I shut my eyes and tensed my sweaty right hand, pulled it back and swung wildly.

It landed squarely. Jake went down.

Holy shit.

My first instinct was to bolt, but my legs weren't cooperating.

From the sudden jumble of gasps and groans behind me, I made out the frenzied voice of Goliath's goon, Kyle McKinney, yelling, "Hit him! Hit him!" But Jake stayed put on the ground, confused, whimpering, covering his bleeding nose.

"Hit him again!" his pal shouted. Shocked, I realized he actually wanted *me* to beat up his best friend. Could it be? Was everyone as sick of Jake's bullying as I was? Or was it that the rush of fighting was so intoxicating that even his most loyal subjects savored the drawing of blood over their friendship?

I shook the thought out of my head and fell hard on that bastard Jake Reilly with eight solid years of Catholic school retribution on my mind.

Adrenaline pumping, I pinned him down with my knees, pulled back my fists, and slammed them into his face again. And again. And again.

Sobbing, he cried, "Stop! Stop! I quit. You win." Streams of tears shined crimson on his bruised cheeks.

I rose to my feet and wiped my bloodied, swollen knuckles across my T-shirt. "You owe me ten bucks" was all I could mutter through a mouth that was empty of any saliva. I turned to leave, though my wobbly legs were barely able to carry me, and I thought for a second that I might pass out right there in front of the whole stunned eighth grade class. Then I inhaled deeply as the faint sounds of hooting and hollering filled my ears.

The giant lay defeated before me.

The next morning, my classmates swarmed around me the moment I got to school. My once nonexistent stature had grown to epic proportions overnight: I'd become the Bully Slayer. Even the popular kids who'd ignored me for the last eight years looked up to me because I'd taken down one of their own. Not to mention I was ten bucks richer.

I was drunk with my newfound significance. Suddenly, I wasn't the weird Italian kid who spent all his after-school free time with his elderly grandparents in their Blue Island "ghetto" instead of the stale upper-middle-class confines of this Oak Forest suburbia. For a brief moment, I wasn't the little boy with the peculiar mom and dad who couldn't speak proper English, who owned a beauty shop and brought their kid sloppy lunches in oil-stained paper sacks.

No, I was the tough kid. The most dangerous kid in school, in fact. In all of Oak Forest, even. And if Oak Forest had been any closer to Chicago than the twenty miles away it was, then perhaps the mayor would have even thrown a parade down State Street in my honor.

During my first-period math class, I flexed my fists, silently studying them, trying to take in the reality that these two bruised, balled-up hands had become my ticket to respect and power.

I took this lesson to heart, absorbing it in every fiber of every muscle in my body. It would end up serving me in the years to come as I would help build one of America's most violent homegrown terror organizations.

2

MILES APART

PERHAPS WHO WE TRULY BECOME begins with our parents' emotional state at conception, filtered by our pregnant mothers' dreams for us. Though we know how we begin, with DNA combining randomly, taking some from Dad here and Mom there, that only accounts for the bones—the hair and eye color, nose shape, height, and characteristics by which the outside world recognizes us.

Maybe the real person, the inner being, is determined not by the arbitrary mixing of genes, but by some mystery science has yet to unravel—a metaphysical collision of two souls inviting another soul to come to life.

In my case, the two souls were Enzo Picciolini and Anna Maria Spinelli.

My father, the youngest of six children, had been fatherless since his early childhood growing up in a tiny southwestern valley town near Salerno, Italy, called Montesano Scalo.

After my father's dad passed, my grandmother moved the family from Italy to Chicago to be near a sister who had already immigrated to the United States. So, in 1962, when my father was sixteen, he boarded an overcrowded passenger ship and a month later settled down with his family on the South Side of Chicago, near Midway Airport.

Christian Picciolini, Blue Island, 1978 (Photo by Maddalena Spinelli)

Enzo later enrolled in beauty school and learned enough English from his older brothers to pass his licensing exams. When he was twenty-five, he met my mother, who, like him, was also an Italian immigrant and a hairdresser.

Within six months, they were married. I know little of their courtship. I've seen wedding photographs and old films, but I can't say whether they were in love or just at the age when they both knew the time for marriage had come. I imagine they were both relieved to have found someone with a similar background—someone who understood the trials of being an outsider, of struggling with a language to which you had not been born, with odd customs, and the challenges of building a new life.

And so, in Chicago on a cold and frosty St. Valentine's Day in 1973, I was conceived by two young immigrants torn between two lands. Awkward and ill at ease in one country, and far away from the other, they were determined that their offspring would know none of their struggles. Anna and Enzo's child would not suffer language barriers, would get a fine American education, and would have options beyond blue-collar jobs in the great new land in which they had planted their roots. They could never have known then the irony of how their young Italian-American son would grow to resent them for it.

To prepare for my birth, my parents made a drastic and culturally uncharacteristic decision: they stretched themselves well beyond their financial means and bought a house in suburban Oak Forest, ten miles away from Blue Island, the working-class Italian suburb on the southwest edge of Chicago where my mother's family lived.

Nonna Nancy, my mother's mother—the matriarch of our family—and Nonno Michele, my grandfather, had left Ripacandida, their close-knit farming community near the ankle of the Italian boot, seven years earlier, in the mid-1960s, to join the ranks of other Europeans who believed the United States was the land of opportunity. After trying to emigrate for many years—the process made complicated by the fact that my grandfather had served in Mussolini's Italian Air Force during World War II—they finally settled in Blue Island, an urban enclave populated with people much like them—hardworking *Ripacandidese* families who believed in family, old-world traditions, and daily consumption of olive oil and pasta.

My grandparents advised my mother against her decision to move out of the neighborhood. Nonna and Nonno lived in adequate comfort in a friendly community made up of old three-story apartment houses made of cinder blocks and bricks, small gardens overgrowing with bell peppers, herbs, and tomatoes, and basement *cantinas* crammed with aging mason jars of homemade tomato ragù, cured sausage, and bottles of vino. They may have moved to a country full of people with strange customs, rude behavior, and no respect for the old ways, but they believed they had the good sense to live among those who adhered to the right way of life—the Italian way.

Outsiders may have considered Blue Island to be a lower-middle-class town, but it had everything my mother could want: family, friends, sustenance growing in the backyard. Fresh eggs and milk were delivered right to her front door every Saturday morning. Early Italian settlers had even built the St. Donatus parish, named after San Donato, their patron saint back home in Ripacandida. Every year, the congregation threw a huge festival in honor of the saint, a feast that matched the one in Italy for devotion, wine, song, and celebration.

My grandmother couldn't understand why her daughter would want to move out of Blue Island to hoity-toity Oak Forest. "Forest?" she'd mock in her fractured English. It was nothing but fancy split-level houses and manicured lawns. Trees wouldn't dare congregate on all that tidiness, even if there was room left over after all those two-car garages were built. Why would families need two cars to begin with? The whole notion didn't make sense to her. In Nonna's eyes, my mother would be paying more for substantially less. Besides, where would they get the money? It wasn't like

Anna and Enzo were going to be able to afford it on the money they made from giving perms to old ladies.

My mother consoled Nonna with the promise that she would bring me back to Blue Island every day. "Now that the baby is a few months old, I'm going back to work doing hair with Enzo, and you will care for him while we're away. Not a day will go by that we won't see you, and Christian will know you as well as he knows us."

So began, when I was barely a couple of months old, a routine that lasted for the first five years of my life. Every morning my mother strapped me into a car seat, raced over to Blue Island, dropped me into Nonna's waiting arms, and hurried off to work at the modest hair salon she and my father had opened near Oak Forest after I was born. Half a day later, either she or my father, or both of them, would come back to swoop me up, eat dinner with my grandparents, put me back into my car seat, and rush back home. As an infant, I was usually asleep by the time we reached the house, and I imagine it must have been confusing for me to wake up in one place and spend the rest of the day in another, only to wake up again in the place I had begun the day with no memory of how I got back there.

I never considered who played what role in my life and whether or not the various adults in it were going about things the right way. Nonna provided the nurturing and guidance a mother normally would, and it never struck me as odd that she was actually my grandmother. And just as Nonna played the role of mother while my parents were busy working, the fatherly responsibilities fell to my grandfather, Nonno. I spent hours at his side, watching him saw wood and pound nails. A master carpenter, he showed me how to hold a nail just right. I trusted him so completely that it never once occurred to me that the hammer he swung could hit my finger instead of the nail I held in place for him.

My grandparents played a huge part in raising me, and it was the sturdy, two-story brown brick building they owned in Blue Island, not my parents' cookie-cutter tract house in Oak Forest, that I considered home.

But, despite having grandparents who gladly took me in and kept their watchful gaze on me, as a young child I longed for my mom and dad. I worried at times that their absence was punishment for misbehaving, so I became the good kid, working hard to give them every reason to want me around. I picked up my Matchbox cars without being asked. I kept my clothes off the floor to keep my room tidy. I didn't leave my soccer ball where my mother or father could trip on it. And I made sure to say "thank you" and "please" and tried to eat everything on my plate.

Still, it wasn't enough. I simply couldn't compete with their steadfast pursuit of the American Dream.

When the time came, my mother made sure to find a school equal to the fine mind she was certain I possessed. Early on, she decided I would become a doctor—both wealthy and respected—and searched diligently for proof she had judged correctly.

But my future as a doctor was not the only factor that made her resolute in her desire to ensure I was well educated. Her own schooling experience had been less than stellar. She had come to America with her family in 1966 not knowing a word of English, during what would have been her high school years. Blue Island's public high school, Dwight D. Eisenhower High, had been a disaster for her. Totally indifferent to the traumas a foreign student might face, the school had no classes, tutors, translators, or resources to help a non–English speaker—or her family. Anna, a simple sixteen-year-old girl from a tiny hamlet in Italy who could neither read, write, nor speak English, was on her own.

Instead of helping her adapt, the other students did what young students desperate to belong themselves do best: they called her names, threw snowballs at her at the bus stop, made fun of her hand-me-down clothes, and mimicked her parents and their backward ways.

My mother lasted less than a year in high school before she dropped out and never went back.

She vowed to herself that her child would grow up knowing all about fitting in and belonging. People would respect him, even look up to him.

Of course, it all depended on where he got his education. He would have to go to one of those nice private schools.

St. Damian Elementary School and its adjacent namesake church spanned the length of the football field that sat behind it. The long, low, blond brick building that encompassed the Catholic parish was huge in my five-year-old mind. Inside, the heavy wooden doors to each of the classrooms were closed, making the narrow, desolate hallways dim and dreary. The heels of my mother's Italian shoes *click-clack*ed like my grandfather's tack hammer as we found our way to the principal's office. The chairs the ancient head nun offered us seemed unnaturally tall, and my feet dangled high above the floor. My mother perched on the edge of her chair, her leather purse clutched tightly in her hands. Her hair was stylishly swept to one side, her makeup appropriately minimal for a meeting with a nun.

The principal, Sister Lucinia, smiled at me, leaning over her formidable metal desk. "I hear you'll be starting school this year, young man," she said, peering down at me through large round spectacles that magnified her eyeballs like giant glass marbles.

"Yes, Sister," I replied, looking her in the eye as my mother had taught me.

"And is this the school you'd like to go to?"

"Yes, Sister," my mother answered for me.

Sister Lucinia continued to ask questions, and we continued to say "Yes, Sister," for what seemed to me an hour or more, but which was probably less than ten minutes.

Finally, the principal turned to my mother. "We are happy to have your son join us, my dear," she said with a wide, wrinkled grin. "He is clearly a bright child. He will be president someday."

I waited for my mother to correct her, to tell her no, I would be a doctor, but instead she clutched her purse so tightly that even the hair dye that had permanently stained her fingertips turned white. "The president? Of America?"

"Yes," the old nun said, winking at me. "The president."

The children who filled the long, dark halls of St. Damian, I would learn inside of a week, weren't anything like the ones I knew in Blue Island.

They didn't eat spaghetti with clams for dinner. They ate noodles and fish sticks. They drank Pepsi with their meals, not homemade wine. They lived in single-family homes, which they would move out of when they were eighteen to go to college and get a degree in accounting to take with them when they moved away and got married and bought their own houses and had kids who ate noodles and fish sticks. The priest at the church said mass in English, not Italian. And they had no idea that the annual St. Donatus festival was the highlight of the summer.

I learned pretty quickly to keep to myself. Without the joys of friendship, school meant boring books and too much praying and itchy uniforms and stupid rules about tucking in your shirt. And like all the other kids who were unfortunate enough to be judged as "different," I was picked on by Jake Reilly—who, I understood the moment I stepped into the first grade, was the kid loudly calling all the shots. But I kept my thoughts to myself, rationalizing that this school didn't matter. These kids didn't count. Blue Island and anyone connected with my life there were the real world, and nobody in this school was any part of that. School was nothing more than a place I had to endure until my mother or father took a break from work to pick me up and drive me to Blue Island, where I belonged.

Throughout the early years of grade school, my life followed a predictable, well-traveled path. During the week I attended classes at St. Damian, and I spent evenings and weekends with my maternal grandparents in Blue Island, usually drawing or playing detective by myself in their enormous, dusty coat closet, which offered me the perfect space to create a fantasy world of my own.

Through a small rectangular window built inside the large closet, I admired the Blue Island neighborhood kids as they careened by on bikes with magnificent steel handlebars and long, glittery banana seats. I'd watch them ride without using their hands as they made their way to friends' houses, drop their bikes carelessly on the sidewalk, hop up the stoop two steps at a time, and bang on the door to summon their pals. Within heartbeats, the screen door would fly open, the friend would appear, they would jump on bikes together and off they'd go, disappearing down an alley, slowly swallowed up by the horizon.

Ultimately, I suspected, they'd pedal to the St. Donatus church parking lot which even I, a lonesome refugee from a faraway land, knew held the life force of every kid who called the East Side of Blue Island home—the unofficial playground, football field, Wiffle ball stadium, and rendezvous spot for every youngster around.

Sometimes I'd practice making friends with the other kids on the block while I rode alone on my little red bike or sat by myself in the closet drawing Snoopy and the other *Peanuts* characters in my sketchpad. Nestled beneath the moth-riddled parkas and coats of seasons past, I'd imagine myself knocking on someone's door, or that my grandmother would send me to a neighbor's house for some sugar, and one of the kids would answer my knock and invite me in to play. While I sat pensive and alone in the closet, I'd find myself unexpectedly pausing, Crayola marker held midair while I pictured someone dropping their bike by the back door and asking Nonna if I was around and if I could come out and play.

But I knew it wouldn't happen. The kids in Blue Island had each other—they went to school together, probably copied each other's homework, maybe even passed love notes in class to girls with names like Gina and Maria, who dotted the i's in their names with little hearts and smiley faces.

They were all such good friends, a tight-knit group of pals. Wild, even, throwing tomatoes and snowballs at passing cars, hopping fences. Laughing. Having fun together.

I'd been entertaining myself, sitting solitary in my grandparents' coat closet for years, but now I desperately wanted to be a part of something. And I wasn't. I was dangling between two worlds ten—or in some ways five thousand—miles apart.

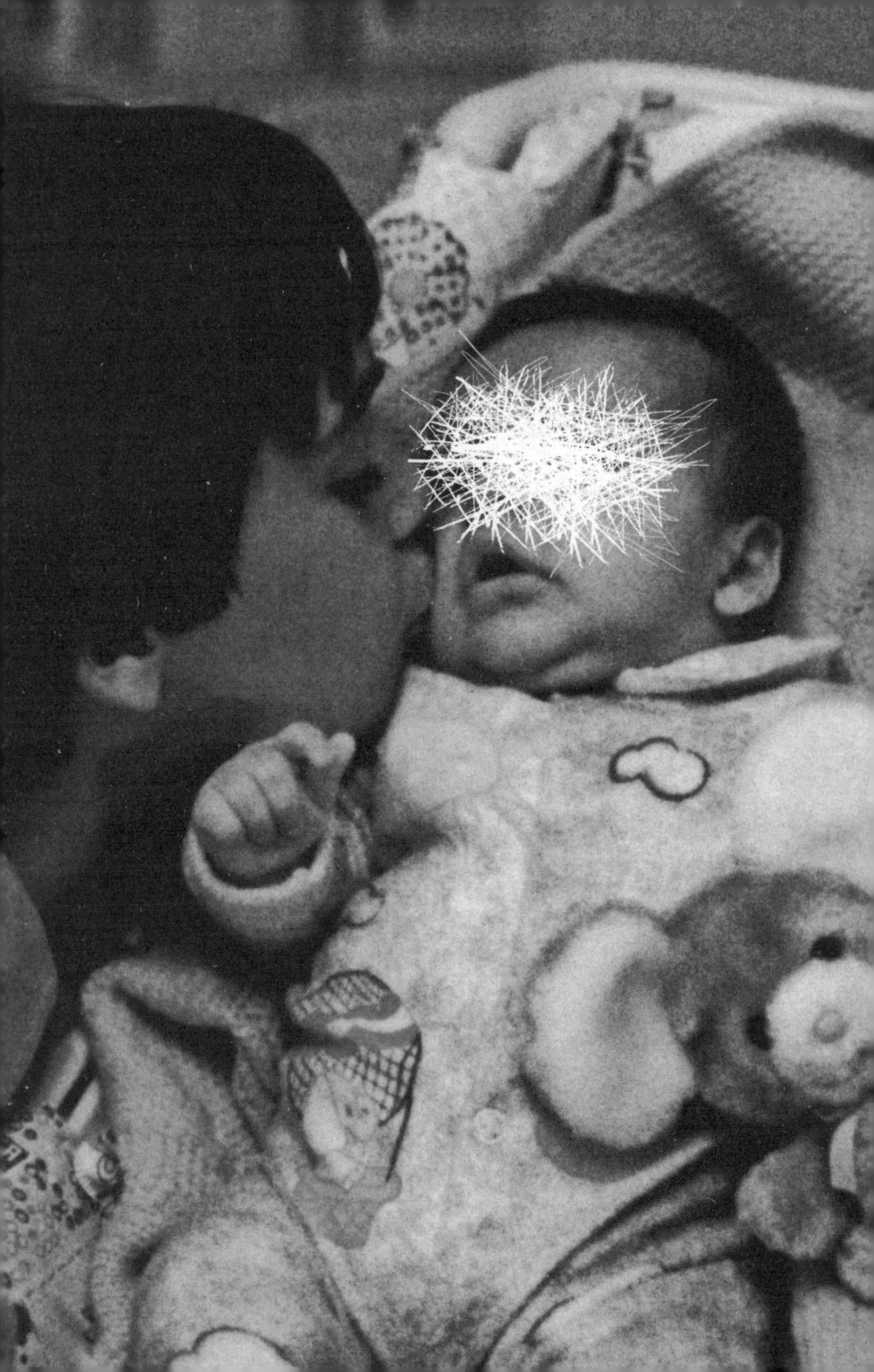

3

BUDDY

By the time I was in sixth grade, I could no longer bear the stigma of being an outcast at St. Damian. I loathed it so much I actually stooped to praying every day around lunchtime. The other kids bought hot meals from the school lunch lady or had colorful tin lunch boxes full of homemade cookies and ham-and-cheese sandwiches prepared by their moms. My mother was often rushed to get to work in the mornings, so she'd show up during lunch period with something she sped to buy through a fast food window between doing a hairstyle and rolling a perm.

Shortly before the bell rang for lunch every day, I'd close my eyes and pray—turning to the false hope the nuns gave us that God watched out for us if we humbled ourselves to ask for help.

"Dear God, if you're really out there, just this once please pay attention. I know there are probably a whole lot of other sinners down here, but I'd appreciate it if you'd ignore all of them but me this afternoon. Hear my prayer, oh Lord, and you can take the rest of the day off. I'm not asking for anything huge like a Sony Walkman. I only want one simple thing."

I paused for a minute to give the Big Guy a chance to realize how little

Christian Picciolini and Buddy, 1983

I was asking for. "Please, God, I beg you, don't let my mother show up with another McDonald's Happy Meal at lunchtime today."

But these words apparently never had enough time to travel from my mouth to His ears because every day, like clockwork, when the bell rang and my class streamed into the lunchroom to eat, there my mom would be, stationed at the door, hurrying toward me, her long leather jacket looking stylish to nobody but herself and her blond hair sticking out at odd angles because she'd rushed out of the beauty shop in the middle of a self-dye job. Her high-heeled boots would hit the polished linoleum floor with sharp staccato notes, tapping out my impending doom.

This particular day was no different. Jake Reilly tripped me as we lined up for the cafeteria. "What's for lunch, Lick-my-weenie?" he sneered. "Your mommy coming today to bring you another little baby Happy Meal?"

When the bell rang I prayed she wouldn't be in the hall, but there she was. She broke into a wide grin, her arms outstretched toward me, the grease from the fries already seeping through the box and onto her black Isotoner gloves.

"Shit," I said, loud enough for Kathleen O'Hara to hear. She'd tell on me for sure for swearing. "Goddamnit," I added, for good measure. If prayers didn't work, maybe curses would. Maybe God would strike me dead.

But no such luck. My mother was upon me, yanking my hand out of my pocket and thrusting the sad, soggy box into it.

Maybe my prayers needed to be more specific. Maybe I should have said, "Dear God, Jesus, Mary, and Joseph, and all the holy saints: don't let my mother or father or anybody they know who owes them any favor or who works in their beauty shop or who came from Italy or who even knows somebody from Italy or has dark hair for that matter or speaks in a funny accent come anywhere near me carrying any food for my lunch. I'm not that hungry, and anyway Dickie Cooper owes me his chocolate pudding because I forged his father's name on the test he failed last week. Amen."

"*Kreestyan*," my mother trilled, her heavily accented voice nasal from perpetually inhaling various hair-coloring products, "Did you think I forgot your lunch today? What kind of *mamma* would do that? I came all this way to give it to you, but now I have to hurry back to the shop and get Mrs. Foster out from the dryer, or her hair will dry and fall out."

Behind me I could sense Jake Reilly snarling, strands of dangling drool beginning to form puddles at his feet. I'd been ducking him for weeks—both literally and figuratively—and now I sensed that my goose was finally cooked. Like smelling salts, the Chicken McNugget aroma had awakened the beast.

At the same moment every day, I wished I didn't have a mother. Who needed one? Or a father, for that matter. I wished they'd go back to Italy and let me fend for myself, or that they'd at least let me move in with my grandparents. I could go to school in Blue Island. I couldn't understand why they wanted so badly to fit in with these people. We weren't like them. We didn't have money like they did.

Thankfully, as soon as the bell rang at three o'clock I could leave them all behind. The bratty kids and snobby parents. My own parents. The priests. The nuns. The prayers. The God who would send me to hell if I ate meat on Friday.

Come three o'clock, I'd be out the door and in a car headed to paradise.

When the final school bell rang later that afternoon, I hung back and daydreamed about what the weekend had in store. As eager as I was to get to my grandparents' house, I had learned to bide my time. My parents were often the last ones to show up at the end of the school day, owing to the hours of their work.

"You still here, Pick-my-weenie?" Jake Reilly jeered, breaking my reverie, as his mother pulled up in their station wagon.

Yup, still here, I thought to myself. Eventually I saw my dad's silver Corvette pull up. Another trinket we could neither afford nor sustain, but my dad had to have it. It was the cherry atop his slice of the American pie.

His arm shot out as he shoved the passenger door open from the inside. "Hurry up, let's go, I have to get back to the shop," he said, even though I was already half in the car, pulling the door shut behind me.

We didn't usually greet each other. What was the point? My father's thoughts were always somewhere else, and if I had said anything, Frankie Valli or Elvis Presley blaring on the Corvette's tape deck would have drowned my words out. Once, with me in the car, he drove through a flashing railroad crossing gate because he was so distracted. The oncoming commuter train missed us by a hundred feet. We didn't talk about that either.

When I'd told my mother about our narrow escape later that night, my parents got into an argument over it. To vent his frustration, my dad turned on me, yelling and smacking me in the back of the head. My dad wasn't a very imposing guy physically—he was rather short in stature with a round belly and prone to wearing heavy gold jewelry—and his slaps were never hard enough to really hurt me, but having him poke away at my head like that was insulting, infuriating, humiliating.

As we drove to Blue Island in silence, I occupied my time by imagining myself at the helm of a fast spy car watching the earth peel away behind me. Rows of storefronts and industrial buildings, miles of oil-stained highway pavement and cracked concrete, stoplights, and road signs swinging in the breeze zipped by in a blur as my father rushed to deliver me to someone else's care.

My brother's birth on August 8, 1983, changed my life, although it would be many years until that became clear to me.

Having virtually no experience with babies, I didn't have the slightest notion of how small a newborn would be. I hadn't spent a great deal of time thinking about little Alex, but I certainly expected someone larger than the tiny infant my mother held out to me the day he was born. In the back of my mind, I knew newborns didn't walk, but I'd pictured more of a toddler. Diapers, yes. A bottle? Sure, babies drank from them. But a tiny, blanket-wrapped blue bundle, a sleeping baby all curled up into a ball snuggled so deep inside it I could only make out a crinkly face and the top of a dark, furry head? That image hadn't even been close to the image in my mind.

But it didn't matter. When my mother came home from the hospital with Alex and leaned down and pulled the blanket back so I could get a look, my heart swelled with pride. It was as if I'd known him my entire ten-year life. He was a part of me, and I was a part of him. He yawned and opened his shining brown eyes. I reached out and touched his cheek, soft as the puffy ski vests I'd floated under during my frequent daydreams in the coat closet. Our eyes met in an admiration so pure that nothing existed for a few endless moments but the two of us.

Having a brother, I discovered, had many benefits. For one thing, my mother had taken time off from the beauty shop, so I could spend time getting more familiar with Oak Forest for the remainder of the summer. When school started again, I still spent weekends with my grandparents in Blue Island and had time to ride my bike, but it was easy to get accustomed to staying in one place all week long.

When Alex heard me coming up the steps, he'd scamper to the front door and throw his pudgy little arms around my knees. His crooked little bucktoothed grin was contagious. I'd wrestle and roughhouse with him, my mother telling me to take it easy, feisty baby Alex begging for more. He wanted to do everything I did, so I tried to teach him how to play catch and hit baseballs before he was out of diapers. I sang him songs and drew funny pictures and made up stories about the characters, narrating in playful voices. When he was two, I gave him a My Buddy doll for Christmas. It looked like him, with his straight brown hair, faint freckles on his nose, and a chubby little body that could be twisted in any direction without complaint, always with a smile on his face. And so from that day forward we exclusively called each other "Buddy."

My parents were more attentive to him than they had been with me, perhaps because they were older or because they weren't so preoccupied about making good in a new country. But as they became more aware of his needs, I found to my great appreciation that they did the same for mine, to some degree.

And so I never resented having a little brother. We were pals, comfortable with each other, safe together. We shared a bond neither of us ever doubted would last until the end of time. Buddy filled a huge void in my life. I felt I had a family member who wanted to spend time with me.

No matter how comfortable I became in Oak Forest, my heart, and therefore my real home, remained in Blue Island.

Since Blue Island had been my solitary stomping grounds from the time before I could crawl, I already knew a lot about the neighborhood. Most of the families had come from the same region in Italy, which meant our families talked about each other all the time.

I'd been watching the older kids for a while. I'd seen them playing Wiffle ball in the St. Donatus parking lot, Nerf football up and down

High Street, and strikeout baseball across the way against the brick wall at Sanders School.

They were known around the neighborhood as the High Street Boys because they all lived on the same block. And it was high time I became one of them, no matter that I lived a street over and was a full grade younger.

The hardest one to win over, I figured, would be Dane Scully. Mr. Popular. He was athletic, the first person I'd ever seen do tricks on a skateboard. All the girls loved him. But he didn't pay all that much attention to them, even when they showed up to his Little League games just to watch him play. I thought he might see we were alike because neither of us had brothers or sisters close to our age, although he was the much younger sibling, instead of the much older one like me.

There were two cousins on High Street who acted like big shots: Little Tony Gianelli and Big Tony Gianelli. Little Tony was good at sports and was the unofficial leader of the High Street crew. Unlike Little Tony, Big Tony was tall and lanky and usually one of the last ones picked for a team because he had about as much athletic ability as a lawn chair. Not only were they cousins and shared the same name, they were born the same year and lived right across the street from each other. Neither had a reputation for being particularly agreeable, so I wasn't sure they'd want me around.

Chuck Zanecki was tall and skinny. He lived across the street from Little Tony, and I felt sad for him when I learned his father had died in a horrible work accident at the local oil refinery. A constant jokester, Chuck was quick to play tricks on people—switch gloves in the dugout, put shaving cream in people's hats, that type of thing—but had a good heart. Of all the kids on the block, he was the only one I thought might possibly—maybe—want to be my best friend.

I didn't exactly have a plan about how I was going to make friends with these guys. I guess I figured if I hung around nearby and talked to them more, it had to happen eventually. So that's what I did.

After watching a baseball game at the park, I'd ride up to High Street on my little red bike and fall in with them, not saying much, but I listened to them talk and once in a while I'd say a few words. When I saw them playing softball in the St. Donatus parking lot, I'd jog out to the outfield to shag a few balls and would join the game by default. I played alongside them more than with them, but to me that was the same as being friends.

Almost.

Little Tony liked to ridicule me. He'd put me in my place when I tagged him out by making fun of my little bike. In fact, everyone made fun of my bike. They also mocked me for my small size, for not living in the neighborhood, for going to a "rich kid" school.

They were going to make me prove myself.

I reached my limit the day I rode up to a serious game of Wiffle ball already in progress.

"Well, if it isn't little baby Christian," Little Tony mocked, punctuating his comment by hawking a loogie on the asphalt. The spit wasn't personal. We all did that as much as we possibly could. In fact, we had a spitting fascination—saliva, sunflower seeds, gum, anything we could get in and out of our mouths.

"Nice bike there," Scully chided. "For a midget." The guys cracked up.

I swung my leg over the bike and let it drop to the ground. "Can I play?" I asked, ignoring their jabs.

I'd posed this question a dozen times before, as had everybody else who showed up once a game was in progress, but this time my question brought laughter.

"Game's locked," taunted Little Tony.

"Locked tight," Big Tony reiterated, spitting.

"Ha! Cool toy bike," Chuck Zanecki cut in.

That did it. I was sick to death of them making fun of my bike and pointing out it was pretty small for a twelve-year-old.

Without another word, I picked up my bike in one hand and took the steps of the adjacent church building two at a time. When I reached beyond the uppermost stair, I spun around on my heel, mounted the offending bicycle, pedaled as hard and fast as I could, and when I hit the landing at the top of the steps, I released my grip and leaped off. The little red bike soared through the air as I watched, transfixed, feeling both thrilled and pained that I was destroying some intrinsic part of me. Before I could blink, my once-beloved red bicycle crashed against the pavement, bouncing on every third stair on its way down to the parking lot below. A small part of my heart broke as what had once been my passage to freedom somersaulted down the steps, hitting the asphalt hard enough to snap the chain.

I bolted to pick it up again, my cold eyes meeting the stunned silence of the High Street crew.

Again I climbed the steps and tore toward them with the little red bike at my side, running even harder, more furiously this time, letting it coast from the top of the landing.

When the bike tumbled down the steps and smashed to a stop the second time, the hushed silence erupted into howls, and Little Tony, Big Tony, Chuck Zanecki, and Scully ran up after me.

In a wild frenzy, we took turns throwing what was left of the bicycle down those stairs over and over and over until the crimson paint stained the church steps like blood and the pedals and handlebars fragmented away from the frame.

The shattered pieces of my childhood lay scattered across the St. Donatus parking lot.

I didn't know it yet, but that day I had become one of the High Street Boys.

A month later when I was riding back from a pickup baseball game, a group of three black kids from the other side of Blue Island stopped me and beat me up. They stole the brand-new black-and-red Schwinn with mag wheels I'd just bought a month before with my thirteenth birthday money. I don't remember much from that day, except I was angry and disappointed in myself for not doing more to protect my new bike from them. Rage swept through me that someone could come into my neighborhood and take what belonged to me.

I got a black eye over it, but my pride was hurt more than anything. My mother was incensed anyone would do that to me, my father berated me and punctuated his words with slaps to the back of my head, saying I was stupid for getting my new bike stolen, and my baby brother cried because somebody had punched me. I had to keep reassuring Buddy my eye didn't hurt in the slightest, it only looked bruised.

A couple of days later some stoner kid from the West Side of Blue Island told me he'd seen the bike in a shady apartment complex on the outskirts of town, so I went over to check it out. Sure enough, I saw my bike on a third floor balcony in a row of apartment houses we considered the "Blue Island Projects."

Without thinking of the potential consequences of my actions, I flew up the stairs and pounded on the door. A black man more than twice my size and at least ten times stronger opened up.

"Damn. Why you be bangin' like you da muhfuggin' cops, white boy?"

"That's my bike on your balcony, sir," I told him. "I'd like it back."

He looked puzzled for about three seconds before bellowing out a boy's name.

The boy, who I took to be his son, appeared faster than I could come up with a plan if he denied the allegation. This giant of a man lunged for his son, grabbing him by the collar.

"Dis white boy say dat's his bike out there. Dat true?"

The kid must have known there was no point in lying, because he immediately nodded and recoiled. *Whack!* His dad backhanded him so hard he fell down. Without missing a beat, he yanked the kid back to his feet and smacked him again. I stood there watching, my mouth open, torn between feelings of vindication and regret. I didn't think it was right to hit a child that way, but then again, the kid and his friends had beat me up, and I had one nasty black eye to prove it.

Once this towering man had reduced his kid to a crumpled, wailing heap on the floor, he stepped over him, walked out to the balcony, and came back with my bike.

"Be more careful wit' it next time," he told me. I didn't dare point out the injustice of blaming me for something his kid did. I'd seen the power of his fist and sure didn't want to be on the other end of it.

The real impact didn't sink in until I showed up to school on Monday. I'd expected everybody in my eighth grade class to make my puffy black eye the butt of their jokes, but instead they studied me like some artifact. They weren't particularly interested in knowing who won; the mere fact I'd been involved in a fight serious enough to end up with a gnarly-looking black eye elevated me out of obscurity and placed me on a momentary pedestal.

My bike had taught me about the exhilarating power of aggression; my story of how I'd gotten the black eye showed me the influence violence has over people.

Moving to Blue Island was no big deal.

Moving to Blue Island was a *huge* deal.

It was no big deal because I had considered it my real home for most of my life.

It was a huge deal because now I got to hang out with my new High Street pals every day. No way could I ever again be considered an outsider.

I belonged.

I graduated in 1987 from St. Damian, bloodied its proverbial nose and flipped Oak Forest off on my way out of town, ready, at last, to be where I belonged, with people like me, both Italian and American, almost each and every one of us.

Oi
Oi
THE FINAL SOLUTION
THIS IS WHITE NOISE
The music of the Skinhead is a most powerfull, hard driving style of Rock N Roll we call "Oi". Oi is nothing like Punk Rock, Hardcore or Heavy Metal. Oi stands alone in classification with its crisp beat and melodic tune variation. Oi is for warriors
FOR RACE AND NATION
SKIN
HEADS
Stronger than Before
ROMANTIC VIOLENCE
P.O.Box 431
Blue Island, IL
60406
WHITE POWER
ROCKNROLL
Sick shit!
-there is a band with guts!
DEAD REDS
Send Names & Addresses OF Commies To:
COMMUNISM IS JEWISH!
ADOLF HITLER
Romantic Violence
P. O. Box 431
Blue Island, Illinois 60406
BACK WITH A BANG
MARCHING MUSIC
R. ROCK AND ROLL MU
BAND IN THE WES
ALL OVER EUROPE,
RISINGS IN GERM
CRANKED ALL THE
ARTIES AND PERS
BY THE FAT CATS A
QUANTITY. ORDER
TODAY FOR ONLY $7
WHITE POWER
ROCKERS UNITE AGAINST COMMUNISM IN CHICAGO
A NEW BREED OF HEROES HAVE SPRUNG FROM THE MIDWESTERN SOIL, BRAVE SKINHEAD PATRIOTS READY TO FIGHT FOR RACE AND NATION.
THESE TALENTED MUSICIANS AND COURAGEOUS WARRIORS HAVE PUT TOGETHER WHITE POWER LYRICS WITH AN ENERGETIC BEAT TO PRODUCE THE BEST AMERICAN SKINHEAD ANTHEMS.
THE FINAL SOLUTION
Chicagoland
Oi
TO HELP THE CHICAGO AREA SKINHEADS SPONSOR WHITE POWER ROCK BANDS SEND DONATIONS OR PURCHASE HIGH QUALITY CASSETTE TAPES OF U.S AND ENGLISH WHITE POWER ROCK BANDS THROUGH;
ROMANTIC VIOLENCE
P.O. BOX 50317
CICERO, IL. 60650
1. SKREWDRIVER 24 SONG TAPE
Oi The word means "hey" in London cockney slang. It refers to a British social and sound movement that has been characterized as "music to riot by."
THE WHITE BACKLASH!

4

WHITE POWER

CARMINE PATERNO HAD BEEN ONE OF MY IDOLS since I was old enough to have one. His father was Nonno's best friend, so Carmine had been at least a small part of my life in Blue Island for as long as I could remember. He was brash and boisterous and stood proud at not much more than five and a half feet. Stocky. Built like an American bulldog, his demeanor was no less fierce. He played the drums and drove a muscle car. He was six years older than I was, and if I could have had a big brother, I would have picked Carmine.

Carmine always thought to pay attention to me when he and his father visited with my grandfather over beers in the garage that served as Nonno's workshop. I admired his devil-may-care attitude. He never treated me like I was beneath him simply because I was younger. He swore when I thought swearing was a sin, and smoked and drank openly in front of adults when I was still buying candy cigarettes and root beer from the corner store on High Street.

"Is that a tattoo, Carmine?" I asked when I saw the fresh ink on his arm.

The new design was a burning torch wrapped with a banner and some

Various Romantic Violence, CASH, and Final Solution flyers, circa 1987

words I couldn't make out. "Yeah, I just got it last week," he replied after draining his Old Style can of its last drops of beer.

"What does it say?" I asked, wide-eyed, trying to get a closer look.

He lifted his sleeve to show me the full design. "It says, 'The Power and the Glory.' It's the name of a song by a band from England called Cockney Rejects."

I thought the band's name was funny, but I didn't dare laugh at Carmine. "That's sweet!" For the rest of the afternoon I hung out behind the garage singing to myself what I thought the chorus might be for a song with that name.

By the time I was thirteen, Carmine had firmly established himself as one of the coolest guys on the whole East Side of Blue Island.

My pal Scully, one of the High Street Boys, lived directly across the alley from Carmine and was mentored by him into ever-deepening levels of defiance. With his finger firmly on the pulse of underground music, Carmine would make Scully bootleg cassette copies of albums from the best punk bands the moment they hit the Chicago scene—The Effigies, Naked Raygun, Bhopal Stiffs, Big Black, Articles of Faith.

Those dubbed mixtapes got Scully and me hooked on punk rock music, and we began to collect vinyl albums of any punk bands we could get our hands on, local or otherwise, competing to buy every new release and imported record we were lucky enough to come across.

Scully seemed to find out about those bands first, thanks primarily to Carmine. Anybody he thought was worth listening to won our immediate respect. Cockney Rejects. The Clash. Ramones. The Pogues. Stray Cats. Joan Jett and the Blackhearts. Angelic Upstarts. X. Sham 69. Combat 84. The 4-Skins. The Business. Cock Sparrer. Bad Religion. Social Distortion.

Scully and I drew the bands' names and their logos all over our ripped jeans, white tees, and Chuck Taylor high-tops. When my mom found my marked-up clothes she threw them out, sure they would turn me into a delinquent. So I learned to hide them. Before I left the house, I tossed them out my bedroom window and changed in the alley before going anywhere.

Punk rock became part of the lives of its devotees in a way that outsiders, especially adults, never understood. It spoke to us and allowed us to speak when we didn't feel we had a voice. It was uncensored and raw and proved it was okay to be lonely or angry or confused about being a teenager in the world. Music was the common link allowing us all to see we were not lost and alone. In it we found each other, and through it we collectively directed our teen angst at a grown-up society we saw as intolerant of us.

The punk scene provided us with an alternative to corporately manufactured mass culture, and it promoted individual creativity and personal action, albeit through rebellion. Through punk lyrics we found release from the pressures of growing up. Watching our parents, we caught depressing glimpses of who we were sentenced to become. Slam-dancing—moshing—to the driving rhythms was an outlet for our anger, frustration, and insecurities. It was exciting to be a part of something in the mid-1980s that wasn't characterized by conformity, Top-Siders, neon popped collars, and endless brown corduroy everything. Punk rebellion felt natural, right, important, alluring.

Naked Raygun concerts were our go-to reprieve from the ordinary. Hailing from Chicago, the band performed in clubs and rented halls, and Scully and I attended every concert we could. It hardly mattered where they were playing, we'd hop on a train to the North Side of the city and go to a five-dollar all-ages show at Cabaret Metro or sneak our way past the bouncers into an adults-only gig at Club Dreamerz or the Cubby Bear.

The concerts were exhilarating. Colorful Mohawks, combat boots, and ratty clothes riddled with safety pins were the fashion mainstays for the hundreds of embittered punks who crammed the venues they played.

The energy in the band's songs was electric, and the crowd swayed as if the surge of power had lit a fuse and ignited our collective aggression. Our sweaty bodies, driven into each other by razor-sharp guitars and wild drumbeats, pulsed and swirled in unison, packed like sardines in front of the stage. A never-ending stream of willful youths clad in bullet belts and studded denim jackets dove from the edge of the stage into our eager arms in the pit where we awaited their tumbling, sweat-slippery frames. The electric energy in the room was profound, and we felt alive with every distorted power chord.

Along with Naked Raygun, Carmine also blasted music from a group called Skrewdriver all over the neighborhood, and I fell hard for the edgy British punk band the moment I heard them—their tunes and beats, the slick way they dressed, and the raspy voice of Ian Stuart, their gruff lead singer. His songs were different than those of other punk bands, unlike anything I'd ever heard. They brought life to a different and wildly more exciting level. But that was inconsequential. I became too engrossed in the energy of the music itself, and I barely registered their lyrics.

I stand and watch my country going down the drain.
We are all at fault. We are all to blame.
We're letting them take over. We just let 'em come.
Once we had an empire and now we've got a slum.

The day I met Clark Martell was when I was introduced to the ideology of white supremacy. Martell's brash confidence, his swagger, showed me instantly how much I had to learn from him. I'd heard his name around the neighborhood before—most likely from Carmine—but I hadn't paid much attention. Now I made it my business to find out everything I could about him.

I started with the piece of paper he'd handed me. Scrawled on the back was the word "Centurion," but the front side revealed a photocopied flyer for a mail-order service called Romantic Violence that sold Skrewdriver tapes and other music for "white people with guts" through a post office box in Blue Island. The typed handbill described Skrewdriver's tunes as "marching music, fighting music, spirit-scaring white power rock and roll music from the finest white power skinhead band in the West." That was the first time I ever heard the term "white power."

Martell's clothes marked him as a skinhead. Skrewdriver was a skinhead band, and I'd seen what they looked like on the back of Carmine's albums; I'd even seen a couple of skinheads at Naked Raygun shows, so I knew enough to recognize one when I saw one. Carmine told me they were a spinoff from the London punk rock and hooligan subcultures and that some skinheads were about more than just music and causing a ruckus at soccer matches. But I didn't particularly care. I didn't feel called to action by the lyrics dominating their songs, words that spoke about politics, police oppression, war and history, and British unemployment. I didn't relate.

Skinheads dressed sharp. Tough. They looked intimidating and were rowdier than punk rockers. They wore British-made Doc Martens work boots like their factory-worker fathers, slim denim jeans or tailored Sta-Prest work trousers, and thin suspenders they referred to as "braces." They shaved their heads and got tattoos and lived in England and a few other places in Europe, but there weren't many in the United States that I knew of. Except for Blue Island.

I wanted to learn more, so I took the city bus to the mall bookstore and shoplifted a copy of the only book I could find on the topic, appropriately titled *Skinhead*, by a British photographer named Nick Knight. In it, I discovered skinheads, or "skins," first appeared in London sometime in the 1960s among working-class teenagers reacting against hippie culture. Upon further investigation, I learned skinheads were pissed off about the lack of jobs and opportunities to make a decent living, so they rebelled against what they believed were the causes of those problems. They didn't fall for the "flower power" notions of peace and love, and they blamed everyone from politicians to immigrants for their troubles. They shaved their heads, both to distinguish themselves from their hippie counterparts and to keep their opponents from grabbing their hair during their frequent street fights.

While I learned that not all skinheads were violent—many factions just adopted the music and look, not the nationalist politics or aggressive attitudes toward immigrants—I learned those that *were* prone to violence typically attacked gays, upper-class students, and local Pakistanis, who, they claimed, were taking their much-desired jobs. In the early seventies, Scotland Yard cracked down on skinheads in London and more or less put an end to their riotous activities.

For a while.

Then, thanks to Ian Stuart, Skrewdriver's singer, whose lyrics I'd practically ignored as their musical beats pulsed through me, the more radical offshoot of skinheads made a comeback in the mid eighties. Stuart formed a political youth action group called White Noise. That, in turn, led to affiliations with the British National Front, a neo-fascist political organization, and the creation of a right-wing music coalition called Rock Against Communism. Skrewdriver shed their initial punk rock aesthetic and soon became the best known nationalist skinhead band in Europe.

The ideologies expressed in their music found an instant audience with many punks and skins who had become disaffected with the soaring levels of immigration and unemployment in 1980s England. Add to that feelings of marginalization and a strong desire to disrupt a system that seemed the source of many of their problems, and many skinheads adopted more radical ultra-right-wing politics—and the pro–white nationalist skinhead subculture was born.

To exploit the sudden popularity of the band, Skrewdriver left their independent British record label, Chiswick Records—where they were label mates with more mainstream punk acts such as Motörhead and The Damned—and secured a recording contract with Rock-O-Rama Records, a West German record company specializing in edgier and more extreme Oi! music, a British brand of skinhead-style punk rock. As a result of that partnership, Skrewdriver's racist skinhead message began reaching throughout all of Europe and Canada, and their music then became available through Martell's mail-order service in the United States.

Carmine told me Martell had even arranged for Skrewdriver to come to the United States to perform, but the plan was foiled when several members of the band couldn't acquire travel visas because of their criminal records. Martell, with Carmine's help, settled for being the sole conduit to import Skrewdriver and other Rock-O-Rama records into the United States. And so, the Romantic Violence mail-order service became the first to distribute white-power music in America.

It was 1987, and while I'd seen a handful of skinheads—some even non-racist, some even black and Asian—throwing kids around in the pit at Chicago punk rock shows, I'd never actually met one in person. That's because Carmine and this guy who'd smacked my head, having borrowed and adopted the style in 1984 from their radical British counterparts, were only two of a few dozen existing in America.

"Be glad Clark took an interest in you," Carmine told me. "He knows what's going on. He's sick of watching white people lose ground to all the affirmative action job discrimination bullshit and seeing minorities mess up clean white neighborhoods like Blue Island. He does something about it too. Doesn't sit back and let shit happen."

"How does he feel about Italians?" I asked clumsily.

"What, you don't think Italians are white?" Carmine laughed. "Who do you think taught all those fucking pasty krauts and limeys to be civilized? If it weren't for the Roman Empire and its fifteen-hundred-year rule, most of Europe would still be living like savages and have black skin like the invading nigger Moors of Northern Africa. Thanks to us Italians, ethnic Europeans today are still white... Italians, Germans, Greeks, English, the fucking Spaniards and the drunk Irish, the Nordics... the whole goddamn lot of us." He pulled out a Marlboro cigarette, lit it, and offered me one.

"Thanks." I took a shallow drag, more interested in what he was saying than the smoke in my hand.

"Even those pansy French bastards," he hacked. "Though, on second thought, maybe we should've let them fuckers go. Regardless, if you're of European heritage, you're on the side of white history. White power! And don't you forget it."

"So Clark's a... white power... skinhead?" I asked, still not exactly clear on what exactly that meant.

"Yeah, but he's more than that. He's a Nazi skinhead, here to save white people from everyone who's trying to destroy us, like the Jews and niggers. After he moved to Chicago from Montana, where he's originally from, Clark worked with the American Nazi Party. But he found that they're a bunch of kooky old white guys who just sit around and complain about how bad things are, so he's using skinhead music to get the message out to younger people. We have a band."

"We?"

"Clark, Shane Krupp, and Chase Sargent... you know them from the neighborhood, right? And me. Final Solution. You've gotta hear us. You'll love it. People are starting to listen to what Clark says about whites needing to watch their backs and fight back."

"Like who? I mean, who's hanging out with him?" I wanted Carmine to keep talking.

"Look around, man. Pay attention. Those shaved heads you see hanging out in this alley aren't some bullshit fashion statement like punk rock has become. They're about showing the world what we're about. Our message is spreading. Word is getting around. And it's starting here, in Blue Island, right before your eyes. We're going to take our country back."

Which of our countries?, I wanted to ask him, but he was already launching into his case for segregation. He and Martell firmly believed in the supremacy of the white race over other ethnicities. He was sick of "muds"—as he referred to all non-white people—moving into quiet white neighborhoods, bringing crime and taking jobs. Martell despised drugs, because he saw them as a tool that blacks and fat-cat Jews with political agendas used to enslave white people, and keep them dumb—docile. "For the last two years, he's been putting together the first white-power skinhead crew in the country," Carmine replied. Leaning forward and dropping his cigarette before crushing it with his boot, Carmine said in an uncharacteristically low voice, "And he's doing a shitload more than that."

I kept digging. "Really? Like what?"

He paused, considering how much I should know. "He's catching heat from the cops for some serious stuff that happened last spring."

Again I pushed for details. But Carmine wouldn't say anything more.

I thought the skinhead look was cool, and their music pumped me up. But, aside from getting roughed up a bit when my bike got stolen, I had no real beef with blacks or even Mexicans—let alone Jews or gay people. To my knowledge I'd never even met any. I was just happy to finally be living in the same neighborhood as my friends.

I didn't see much racism in our community, although, because most families had come from the same small village in Italy, there was an overwhelming amount of hometown pride, and we tended to stick together. When some Mexican families moved onto our block, some of the parents and grandparents weren't too happy about it, and we did hear the occasional "there goes the neighborhood" remarks. But the racial tension that I was aware of seemed to begin and end there.

So was I initially drawn to Martell's racist agenda? Not really.

But he was magnetic. Charming. I wanted to be like him, and like Carmine and the other people I saw them hanging around with. Why? Because Martell was the first adult—even though he was only twenty-six years old when I met him—who had ever disciplined me and provided a valid explanation for doing so. He hadn't asserted his authority without good reason. When he scolded me for smoking pot in the alley, it was because he thought it was bad for me and took the time to explain the consequences; it wasn't merely "Put that joint out, because it's illegal, and I'm an adult, and I said so." This persuaded me that he wanted what was best for my future—so much so that he'd smacked my head. Just like my dad did.

And so I changed my behavior: I swore off weed, even though I had barely been introduced to it. When Martell and Carmine and their friends were in the alley listening to music or monkeying with their cars, I made sure I was in visible proximity. I followed Martell around and observed his mannerisms. His racial rhetoric sank in too. Most of my High Street friends had begun moving away to the suburbs. Was that because Blue Island was less safe now, I started to wonder, with other races moving in? My new bike had been stolen by black kids, after all.

I looked at my neighborhood, family, and friends with wary eyes, questioning all of the things I'd once taken for granted. I'd never liked school, which made it easy to accept that teachers lied to us about history—presented it the way that suited them. Maybe Martell knew something about the way things really worked that they weren't teaching us in school. Maybe he was right when he claimed the people who wrote the history books were all Jews and fed us a bunch of propagandized bullshit.

Aside from my seeing him with Carmine, Martell kept cropping up more and more in neighborhood discussions. His intensity scared people, cops included. Conversations stopped when he walked into a room. That was something I admired. Intentionally or not, Clark Martell had made me a whole new person. I wanted to carry his weight.

By the end of the summer, when Carmine was busy working his job at a local muffler repair shop, Clark would regularly task me with going to the post office or running off copies of flyers and literature for him. He had begun publishing a newsletter called *Skrewdriver News* that he handed out in front of concert venues when trying to recruit punk-rock kids. I'd overdeliver by cheating the copy counts when it came time to pay the cashier. That typically meant we got at least twice what we'd paid for.

Clark would reward me when I did particularly well. He'd give me a pair of his secondhand boots, or a faded Skrewdriver T-shirt, or more music cassettes, which he seemed to have an abundance of. I ate it all up and would squirrel these gifts away so my mom couldn't find them. Then, one day, Clark handed me a tattered red paperback titled *The Turner Diaries*. Until then, for as long as I could remember, I hadn't read any of the books my teachers assigned in school, having faked my way through every book report. But I couldn't wait to read the gift from Clark.

I had been comfortable as a High Street Boy, but now I had awoken to the larger world, and I wanted more than to just fit into it. I wanted to matter. Ever since I was a lonely little kid, playing make-believe in my grandparents' coat closet, I'd felt I would someday be called on to do something truly big. Now I wanted people to look up to me, the way I looked up to Clark, and for as noble a reason—protecting the white race.

Like most people who are caught up in someone's charisma, I looked for evidence that Clark was right, not wrong. I visited bookstores and sat and read books from the shelves, and I took an interest in history and current events. Sure enough, I concluded that giving college scholarships to minorities meant passing over more deserving white kids. I noticed how lots of the people I was coming to know as "muds,"—blacks and Mexicans, mostly—worked labor jobs and in restaurants, which seemed to prove somehow that whites were being shoved aside in favor of lesser-paid undocumented immigrants. In place of trustworthy families from Italy and Europe, strangers with vastly different ways of living had moved in. I soon began perceiving life through Clark's shrewd lens and started to believe Blue Island, my beloved sanctuary, was circled with sharks.

My family and friends didn't listen to my new ideas. My parents weren't concerned. They shrugged me off and changed the subject. That only seemed to make it clear to me how brainwashed into indifference the world had become at the hands of the Jewish-controlled media.

I was about to turn fourteen years old and start high school. Sitting in class all day would only slow me down.

I was already learning about things that mattered. Things most people took for granted.

And I didn't need a classroom or some double-talking teacher to try to change my mind.

Rapidly, living for innocent fun faded, playing Wiffle ball and riding bikes with the High Street Boys didn't seem exciting anymore, and the need to live for a greater purpose came sharply into focus.

5

ROMANTIC VIOLENCE

When my freshman year of high school started in August of 1987, despite my vehement protests, my parents enrolled me in Marist High School, a private, all-boys Catholic school on the South Side of Chicago. I'd scored high on my entrance exam and was given a full load of honors classes. Those I could handle, but the last thing I wanted was more God and saints and prayers pounded into my head.

But on the first day, when I bumped into Sid and Craig Sargent—the two younger skinhead brothers of Chase Sargent, a close cohort of Clark and Carmine—I was ecstatic. I recalled seeing them drinking beer in the alley on occasion and recognized them right away by their cropped hair and the white straight laces in their boots. Even if the school did require them to wear a necktie and slacks, they remained identifiable.

The three of us became fast friends, and a few days later, Craig gave me my first very own Skrewdriver cassette with the *Hail the New Dawn* record dubbed on side A and two short albums, *Boots and Braces* and *Voice of Britain*, on the flipside. While I'd heard Carmine blasting Skrewdriver's music nearly every day, and I knew enough about them from listening to Scully's tapes, I hadn't owned my own copy.

"This is some sick shit! This band knows what they're talking about,"

Craig said, echoing Carmine's sentiment. Despite being in the same grade and only a few months older than me, Craig had been mentored for some time by two older brothers who were skins—Sid and Chase—and already knew the ins and outs of recruiting. Craig was tall and imposing and had the routine down pat. "White people are going to be in big trouble if we don't pay attention to what this band is saying. Just like England, European whites built America, and now we're being pushed aside by the Jews in favor of blacks and Mexicans."

Skrewdriver, and more specifically Ian Stuart, had a real knack for crafting music and lyrics that inspired young people to take action. The band had given birth to the white-power music genre and with Ian Stuart's keen ability to identify and deliver what embittered youths wanted before they even knew they wanted it, it was only a matter of time before his politically infused anthems stood apart from those of his contemporaries in the London punk rock scene and made it to the United States.

Skrewdriver wrote anthems with relatable directives built in, unlike the whiny punk protest songs I'd become used to. The lyrics gave us the truthful education our lying schoolteachers refused to deliver, for fear we'd see through their manipulated account of history. "White Power." "Blood & Honour." "Tomorrow Belongs to Me." "Free My Land." Songs that filled me with purpose and pride instead of childish, nihilistic impulses like punk rock music did.

Armed with my new cassette and a Walkman, I listened to Skrewdriver over and over and over until I heard the words in my head even when my player's batteries had run down.

People try and put you down and stomp you to the ground.
They don't seem to realize that there's no way you'll back down.
There is nothing that they can do to step on you and me,
Because we'll just keep on fighting, that's the way it's got to be.

Again, I turned to my immediate surroundings, half hoping to find evidence that hordes of minorities were messing up Blue Island and nearby neighborhoods. Determined to find evidence to support the claims in the music I was listening to, I began noticing strangers who couldn't even keep their yards clean, who brought junk cars home and left them to clutter up the street. I noticed when black men on the corners dealt drugs. Mexicans, and their hordes of children, along with a dozen other relatives from some Third-World country, were living in crime-riddled housing projects.

Scully waded into the skinhead mind-set with me. We dubbed and swapped more cassette tapes, listening to more Skrewdriver and expanding our collection to other like-minded English skinhead bands. Brutal Attack. Skullhead. Sudden Impact. No Remorse. I took their lyrics to heart. The music was no longer a solitary beat bringing me to a new level of alive—it was both knowledge and prophecy.

We pooled together our holiday and birthday money, purchased bank money orders and books of stamps, and sent away for Ben Sherman and Fred Perry shirts from Shellys, a store on London's Carnaby Street specializing in skinhead couture. By now my body had begun to fill out and grow, and I was no longer shorter and smaller than everyone else my age, which meant that Scully and I could swap clothes and essentially double our skinhead wardrobe.

We set about Chicago to find shiny, steel-toed Doc Martens boots in peculiar Goth boutiques like 99th Floor and Wax Trax. We wore braces, the thin suspenders Clark wore. I rolled the cuffs of my Levis like I'd seen the others do in the alley behind Carmine's, and over a plain black T-shirt I sported a military surplus black nylon bomber jacket purchased from the local flea market. I adorned it with symbolic patches like Celtic crosses and Confederate flags, which I believed were standard issue for any skinhead worth his salt. I turned heads when I walked down the street, as if people were nervous when I was too close. I liked a look that intimidated without my needing to do a damn thing. And people made assumptions about my willingness to fight rather than take shit from anybody.

Scully and I shaved each other's heads in his dingy basement. Concrete floors, exposed pipes, and dangling light bulbs were the ideal setting for us barely teenage boys taking a stand for white working-class adults everywhere.

I shaved his head first. I adjusted the guard on the clippers, not meaning to shave him completely bald. But it was my first time using the shears, and before I knew it, Scully's hair was cut down to his scalp.

He cried. I'm not putting him down for that. I didn't blame him. A pasty bald head was not a great look on him, and he'd have to go to school looking like that on Monday. Maybe the girls would avoid him. Laugh at him even. Shit.

I pulled him to his feet and put the clippers in his hand. Plopping down on the metal folding chair myself, I said, "Go ahead, I messed up your head. Now it's my turn. Take it off. All of it."

So he did.

When my mom saw my fresh buzz cut later that night, she cried. "Oh, my God, Christian, what did you do? Why did you cut off your beautiful hair?" She attempted to caress my head as if the tears welling in her eyes and her pleas to God could magically make it grow back faster. "You look like you're sick and have cancer," she said, sobbing, and she pulled me close. "It's this punk garbage, isn't it?"

I let her grieve, silently burning in the notion that my shaved head really meant I was working on the cure to the multiracial cancer that was eating away at our sick society.

Gone were the days of my pageboy hairstyle. And my youth.

Only four months had passed since I'd met Clark, but we were skinheads now. Literally. Officially.

Politics meant little to Scully. He only liked the look and the music.

So, apparently, did other people.

With my tough new look and shaved head, my popularity soared. Girls liked being around me. I met Jessica Rimbaldi, a cute Blue Island cheerleader who took to wearing a bomber jacket and Docs, and we both soon proudly lost our virginity together.

I was all of fourteen. Life was good.

If it hadn't been for school and my mother—who spied on me and pestered me with constant questions and suspicions—and other signs the white race was about to be annihilated, I would have had no complaints.

But I lost no sleep over the annihilation part. Clark was building a resistance army. He'd already formed the Chicago Area Skinheads—CASH—in 1985. It was the first organized white-power skinhead crew in the United States. Between CASH and Romantic Violence—CASH's growing white-power music mail-order operation—Clark now had a regular following of a couple dozen skinheads in Blue Island and around Chicago. A handful of the original female recruits, like Mandy Krupp—Shane Krupp's sister—and Kat Armstrong, had been Charles Manson worshippers before becoming skinheads. Now they were Clark Martell devotees.

I saw then that Clark's influence was growing. Opposing skinhead crews began popping up around the city, some with a mission to counter his racist advances. The Medusa Skins and Bomber Boys just liked to get drunk and fight mostly and didn't claim a side, but the more outspoken anti-racist factions of skinheads, the Pitbulls and SHOC—Skinheads of Chicago, or the "Antis" as I began to call them, short for anti-racists, lured some would-be white-power skins to their side.

Skinheads scared people. When a bunch of us were together, fights broke out. Bad shit happened. On the eve of November 9, 1987, the week of my fourteenth birthday and the forty-ninth anniversary of Nazi Germany's *Kristallnacht*, when SS storm troopers had raided Jewish stores in 1938, white-power skinheads stormed the North Side of Chicago, smashing in windows of shops they suspected to be owned by Jews and painting bloodred swastikas on synagogue doors.

I hadn't had anything against Jewish people before—in fact, I didn't even know any—but from the materials I'd been studying and Martell's unabashed hatred of them, I had come to the conclusion that Jews were indeed evil masterminds trying to secretly undermine unsuspecting American whites into extinction by pushing their multiculturalist agenda.

Clark was beside me, whispering to two older, long-haired American Nazi Party twin brothers in the alley when I mentioned that it was my birthday. Carmine, who was changing the engine oil on his Firebird, pulled a frosted Old Style can from a Styrofoam cooler in the garage and tossed it to me. "Happy birthday!"

Clark paused his conversation with the mustached twins to approach me and put his hand on my shoulder. "I have something important for you," he said, smiling. "Might be going out of town for a bit to take care of some business. Can I rely on you to check the Romantic Violence post office box and hold the mail for me until I get back?"

"Yeah, of course! You can count on me, Clark," I responded, before the question had even fully escaped his lips. With that he handed me a small brass key and returned to hushed conversation with the two jackbooted men.

I was unaware that Clark didn't know if he'd be coming back. What was inescapable, though, was the utmost importance of what the three men were discussing. I felt the tiny ridges of the key with my fingers and squeezed it tight in my palm, knowing fully this key would unlock more than a mailbox. I had no idea this would be the last time I'd see Clark Martell.

Rumor got around that Clark was behind the *Kristallnacht* rampage, and he was arrested, along with several members of the CASH crew and one of the long-haired American Nazi Party fellows from the alley. It wasn't the first time the police had been after him, either. In fact, it proved what Carmine had told me—the cops, the FBI, maybe even the vigilante Jewish Defense League, were watching Clark's every move.

It wasn't only Clark who was being watched. Carmine was too, and so were Chase Sargent and his brothers Sid and Craig, the Manson Family skinhead chicks, Shane Krupp, and the dozen or so other people I'd seen hanging around in the alley. FBI raids of their houses were becoming pretty standard. Their home phones were wiretapped, and they were routinely tailed and photographed by less-than-subtle law enforcement officers. The Romantic Violence mailbox got monitored. Letters were opened and resealed.

My desire to be part of their group grew the more the signs of surveillance—and the danger it suggested—became undeniable. This was the stuff of mobster movies. Serious good guys and bad guys in action. And while we good guys were being deceptively portrayed as violent thugs by the Jew-run media, this was for the good of a cause: protecting the white race from ethnic genocide. I never wondered why we needed any protection.

"Can you believe it?" I asked Scully when the Chicago *Kristallnacht* story came out in the *Chicago Tribune*. "Clark's not just saying he's going to save the white race. He's actually doing something about it, like Carmine said."

Adolf Hitler hated Jews because he felt they were destroying his beloved Germany and were the cause of his country's intense economic struggle after World War I. He saw Jews as parasites that leeched onto healthy nations throughout history and destroyed them like a cancer. Now Clark was going after them the same way Hitler did, because he saw the same things happening in America at the hands of Jews who ran the media and banking systems.

I was awed to imagine Clark doing this level of damage. He and his followers shook people up, had minorities and Jews locking their doors and putting up "For Sale" signs. I wanted to stand beside him. Average white people were too meek; they needed a leader like Clark Martell to inspire them.

I had the same passion and fury running through me, waiting to be unleashed.

After the news hit that Chicago neo-Nazi skinheads were behind the violence and destruction of Jewish property, the terms *skinhead* and *fear* became synonymous. People began to consider skinheads racial terrorists. In a way, I liked the sound of that word *terrorist.* The power behind it. But people had it wrong. White-power skinheads were patriots, not terrorists. We were fighting battles other whites whispered about but were too complacent to take up.

Honest, hardworking white people like my parents were being forced to work day and night just to make ends meet to support their families, while the minorities sat back collecting unemployment and pumping out more crack babies to boost their monthly welfare checks. My mom often worked three jobs—in the salon, as a caterer, and in the evenings during election season as a vote tabulator. My dad ran the beauty shop all day and looked after Buddy while my mom was away working at night. And when

Buddy grew up he'd have to struggle the same way just to survive. That didn't sit right with me.

All the while, Clark said the Jews enjoyed the turmoil they secretly created as they sat in their ivory towers rubbing their greedy Zionist hands together, watching white and minority pawns finger-pointing at each other while our society declined to their benefit. If scaring white people into submission meant that they'd ultimately see the truth behind the Jewish lies, then Clark was well on his way to opening their eyes.

In January of my freshman year I found out more of what Carmine's hushed innuendos concerning Clark's activities had been about. He and five other CASH skinheads had busted into the apartment of a twenty-year-old woman the previous April.

Angie Streckler had been a CASH skinhead at one point but quit the crew abruptly. Clark and the others had heard she had a black friend—a totally intolerable behavior for a white-power skin. To discipline her, Clark and some of the CASH crew stormed into her place, pistol-whipped her, sprayed Mace in her eyes, and in a Mansonesque tribute, the girls used her own blood to paint a swastika and the words "race traitor" on the walls of her apartment. She'd never reported it, until the cops somehow caught wind of the attack when the group was arrested for the *Kristallnacht* episode and pursued additional charges.

Some other things Clark had done around Chicago before setting up shop in Blue Island in late 1984 came out too, including physical assaults on six Mexican women, the fire-bombing of a minority family's home, spray-painting swastikas on three other synagogues, and perpetrating numerous incidents of vandalism on various Jewish-owned businesses and cemeteries.

From my perspective, he was a fucking legend.

I hungered to talk to Clark again and schemed ways to meet up with him when he got out, but he failed to make bail. He was sentenced to prison for eleven years.

About a month later on a cold February afternoon, less than a year after the Angie Streckler incident, Scully and I settled in with a twelve-pack of Old Style to watch Oprah Winfrey, who was having some white-power skinheads from California on her daytime talk show: Dave Mazzella, Marty Cox, Tom Metzger and his son John Metzger, the leaders of White Aryan Resistance (WAR).

The show's producers were even able to get Clark on the phone to make some comments from prison. While on the line, not only did Clark put the poser Anti skinheads who were in the studio audience in their place by calling them out over the airwaves for their cowardly unwillingness to stand up for their race, he was clearly able to communicate that power-hungry rich people—or capitalists, as he called them—were the real enemy, pitting every race against one another in the name of the almighty dollar and ultimate global control.

And then, right there on national television, for all the country to witness, Cox stood up from his seat and said it was a proven fact that blacks came from monkeys. Oprah was predictably incensed, pushing Cox's arm down when he shoved it forward in a Nazi salute. I couldn't believe my ears. It happened in a split second, but he'd called her a monkey to her face in front of millions. The segment aired repeatedly on news stations across the United States. And I knew beyond a doubt, from that moment on, the white-power movement was going to be staggering. I could feel the American public knotting up with fear, like the visibly panicked people I sat down next to on the city bus. Skinheads weren't a passing curiosity anymore. I stepped up my efforts to be noticed. I dressed the part, talked the talk, and brought up my new ideologies whenever I found the chance, to whomever was in my proximity.

The High Street Boys were preoccupied with high school and weren't into it, and we drifted apart, but I knew something big was coming down.

I checked the post office box religiously and delivered the mail to Carmine. In return, Carmine began supplying me with stacks of photocopied pamphlets blasting everything non-white, some of them quoting lyrics from our favorite bands. I would use these to recruit new skins like I'd seen Clark do.

White-power music was now the only thing I listened to. I let the messages within the lyrics and literature root deep into my soul. They spoke to me, and I listened.

6

FOURTEEN WORDS

SKINHEAD RALLIES, get-togethers in shabby, moldy basements, were better than hanging out in the St. Donatus parking lot with the High Street Boys, as far as I was concerned. Swastikas and racial slogans were crudely spray-painted on crumbling cement walls. Driving music blared. Skrewdriver. Talk of blood and soil and racial holy war. Skinhead girls in plaid miniskirts and fishnet stockings. Beer. Lots of beer, flowing from cans, bottles, and kegs when we could scrape enough money together.

But there were always brawls. Rowdy, drunken scraps. Shoves over a crooked glance quickly advancing to whole crews pummeling each other. Blood flowing. Stomping and kicking. With heavy steel-toed Doc Martens, the results could be brutal.

This part puzzled me. What kind of brotherhood was this? Weren't we all on the same side? We were all on the same team, fighting against massive odds that required us to operate as a single focused unit.

When the High Street Boys had hung out together, we'd spent a lot of time playing team games such as baseball and football. Neighborhood dogs barked, strained to join us, chasing us up and down behind chain-link fences as we streaked past them, and since some dogs would love to sink their teeth into us when balls fell into their yards, we had a steadfast rule that whoever knocked it over the fence had to go in after it. Nobody liked the job, but we all took our turn as both retriever and dog decoy. And we all survived because we had each other's backs.

What I was noticing with skinheads was that we didn't seem to operate this way. It was as if, without a strong voice to guide us, everyone was out for himself.

We needed Clark Martell. I kept these observations to myself, though. It was too early for me to weigh in, but I knew my realization of the situation proved I could be leading this group someday.

I attended every local gathering I heard about, observing and being seen; passing around copies of literature I'd collected from Carmine and Clark; promoting CASH. The remaining older skinheads, many of whom had begun growing their hair out to avoid the increased attention from the police, showed up now and again, and I felt their eyes on me. They knew I was more than just a kid, even if I was only fourteen. I yearned for an opportunity to show them I was their equal, and I wanted to demonstrate it in a big way.

One Sunday morning, Chase Sargent pulled his rusty Cadillac Seville up alongside Scully and me while we were smoking cigarettes in the St. Donatus parking lot and asked if we wanted to go to a meeting with him that afternoon. A rally.

Besides Clark and Carmine, Chase was one of the few remaining original CASH skins. He was tall and gangly, but his reputation as a fighter was second to none, and he also played guitar, two skills I hoped to acquire myself someday. The cool factor was off the charts. We didn't hesitate to say yes when he asked.

Scully and I attended the meeting, held in Mandy Krupp's ramshackle apartment in Naperville, Illinois, a turn-of-the-century settler's village turned manufacturing ghost town about an hour's drive west of Blue Island. We drove up with muscle, Scully behind the wheel of the patchy blue-and-gray 1971 Camaro he'd recently bought on his sixteenth birthday.

We were dressed to kill. Scully wore his dad's old army boots. I polished the pair of boots Clark had given me for a job well done a few months before he went to prison. I had flyered three hundred windshields of the cars parked for a demolition derby at nearby Raceway Park. I knew the patrons who flocked to the Sunday derbies at the racetrack were the types of low-hanging marks Clark could easily convert. It had been my idea to target the event, and Clark rewarded my initiative with a pair of his old, worn-out Docs. They were a little big, but I'd grow into them. In the meantime, I stuffed some newspaper into the toe area. I tore the white laces out of my Adidas gym shoes and laced my new boots with them. I was ready to kick some ass.

Neither Scully nor I spoke much during the drive up. Instead we cranked the car stereo and sang along loudly to a poorly dubbed copy of Skrewdriver's *White Rider* album. Maybe it was nerves that kept us avoiding the obvious conversation. More likely it was because we both knew the road ahead of us was about to swallow us up—and I was thrilled for it to happen.

Close to thirty skinheads, most of whom were in their early twenties, had packed the cramped flat by the time we arrived. Newly minted skins from Michigan, Wisconsin, Texas, and Illinois. Carmine. Chase Sargent. Sid and Craig. I was the youngest; Scully and Craig were the next youngest at barely sixteen. There was hardly room to stand. Clark had been busier gathering recruits than I'd thought. It was a shame he couldn't be there to see the fruits of his labor.

Somebody handed me a cold can of Miller High Life. I was already high on the thrill of being there, but I wasn't about to say no to this display of acceptance. Besides, to tell the truth, the whole thing was a little overwhelming, and some alcohol would calm my nerves. Everywhere I looked were shaved heads, tattoos, boots, braces. People had this down. Nazi and Confederate battle flags doubled as window curtains. Armbands with swastika insignias were plentiful. Some hard-nosed skinhead girls hung on to the arms of some of the bigger guys, making it easy to see who the key players were.

Before I finished my first beer, a large skinhead with a pockmarked face and a thick swastika tattooed on his throat brought the meeting to order. Rising, standing in the corner of the living room, he spoke a simple statement, one I would know by heart by the end of the night. A creed I would live by for the next seven years of my life: "We must secure the existence of our people and a future for white children."

"Fourteen words!" his voice thundered. That statement was a mantra.

Immediately, everyone in the room turned to him, stopping mid-conversation to yell in one voice, "We must secure the existence of our people and a future for white children."

"Do you believe in the fourteen words?" he demanded.

All around the room, arms shot out in Nazi salutes.

"Heil Hitler!" everyone around me cried in unison.

I threw my arm out too, looking sideways at Scully, who appeared unnerved. Not me. This was fantastic.

For more than an hour my heart pounded with purpose, as I stood mesmerized, listening to fiery rhetoric I would soon be able to recite in my sleep.

An upside-down and partially charred American flag hung on the wall beside the speaker as he gripped his beer can firmly and spoke loudly to those gathered. "Our traitorous government would have you believe racial diversity is advanced thinking, brothers and sisters. That all races should live in peace and harmony. Bullshit! Take a look around. Open your eyes and refuse to be fooled. What do you see when niggers move into your neighborhoods? You see drugs and crime pour into your streets, not equality. Your gutters fill with trash. The air starts smelling foul because these porch monkeys don't do anything but sit around and smoke crack and knock up their junkie whores all day.

"Only thing they're cleaning up is all that hard-earned money you and I pay in taxes. Those people are living off welfare, unemployment. First in line for every handout the government can offer. Section eight housing. Free lunch programs at school. The only reason those little welfare kids go to school is to get those free lunches. All paid for by us white people, by hardworking Americans who'd never dream of having our kids eat free meals because we take care of ourselves."

Several thick tattooed necks wrinkled as their shaved heads nodded in agreement with the speaker. He clearly held the room's attention, despite one of the Milwaukee skins retching his guts out loudly in the kitchen sink.

"And while you and me work our fingers to the bone, these parasites are out selling drugs to your little brothers to make them stupid. Selling them junk so their teeth will rot and they'll look sixty by the time they're sixteen. Innocent whites are getting caught in gang crossfire and dying at the hands of these criminals.

"They're making our Aryan women dependent on drugs so they'll whore themselves for a taste of whatever vile substance they've hooked them on. You think they're selling this garbage just to get rich and buy their Cadillacs and gold chains? Get your heads out of your asses, comrades. They're selling this poison to make white kids as stupid as their mud kids. They want our people to become so dead inside they'll smoke and snort everything in sight. Shoot drugs into their arms and between their toes. They want to see our people destroy their brain cells and end up in jails where they'll get violated by these filthy animals who are locked up for murdering and raping innocent white girls.

"And who is leading these degenerates in the destruction of our race? The kikes and their Zionist Occupation Government. That's who!" The speaker launched into a tirade against Jews and Israel that I'd hear at every rally I attended from that moment on, but never with such fervor. The cords on his neck looked ready to tear; spit foamed in the corners of his mouth. His eyes were ablaze with the sensation of truth.

Nobody spoke as he reminded us that Jews and their shadowy Zionist Occupation Government—ZOG, as the movement referred to it—controlled the media and were lying through their gold-crowned teeth trying to pit blacks against whites, Christians against Muslims, so they would kill each other off, leaving nobody but the Jews, who had the ignorant, pretentious belief they were God's "Chosen People." They, of all people, who nailed the goddamn Son of God, Jesus fucking Christ, to the cross. Nine years of Catholic school had even taught me that.

He ended as he began. "Fourteen words, my family! Fourteen sacred words."

On our feet, we shouted those fourteen words over and over and over.

"We must secure the existence of our people and a future for white children! We must secure the existence of our people and a future for white children! We must secure the existence of our people and a future for white children!"

We closed with stiff-armed salutes and ear-splitting chants of *"Sieg heil! Sieg heil! Sieg heil!"*

Adrenaline burned through me like fire, nervous sweat extinguishing it, spreading from head to foot. I was ready to save my brother, parents, grandparents, friends, and every other decent white person on the planet from the utter despair we were facing.

The dank air was thick with personal stories about losing jobs to illegal aliens willing to work for less than minimum wage so they could send the cash back to Mexico to their families of dozens of little "wetbacks" who would, in turn, use the money to smuggle more illegals into the U.S. to take away more jobs from white Americans. There was a graphic firsthand account of a virginal white sister being raped in a school bathroom by ruthless Puerto Ricans for a gang initiation. These hardened skinheads ripped open the conspiracies forced upon us by the Jewish media complex, exposing the lies that money-hungry power brokers heaped upon the ignorant masses to keep them in line while they plotted our cultural demise.

I learned "innocent" Jews hadn't been mass exterminated during World War II. There had been no Holocaust. Some Jews had died, yes, but they were simply necessary casualties of war in a fight against the enemy. Hitler had realized the truth that the Jews were trying to undermine European society by manipulating its financial systems and polluting its beautiful legacy of fine art by pushing degenerate "modern art." He had tried to save his people by identifying the disease and cutting it out. Instead, he'd been vilified by the Jewish press and Communist spin doctors, a hero turned monster under a barrage of lies and distortions.

Scully stood beside me, tense, glancing over his shoulder. "Can we go?" he whispered.

"Are you kidding?" I asked. I was astonished. "Don't you want to know how the world *really* works?"

The crowd broke into another round of ear-splitting "*Sieg heil*" chants, one person after another thrusting out his—or her—arm in solidarity. I joined in.

This was what knowledge was all about. Not being handcuffed to our school desks and forced to learn about the Emancipation Proclamation or the Gettysburg Address. This was the American Revolution. The truth. Right here. Right now. We were losing our God-given rights to minorities and Jews, and as a society we were so clueless and self-satisfied, we were letting it happen right under our goddamn noses.

This meeting, it turned out, was about action. About combining forces and bringing the various scattered skinheads throughout the United States under one unified banner. A drunk from the Confederate Hammer Skinheads crew from Dallas suggested a modified version of their group's name as a name for the new collective. Someone else chimed in proposing that a simple logo with two crossed hammers, similar to those used by Pink Floyd in their movie *The Wall*, could signify strength and the idea of a white, working-class ethic. The group, eager to move on to the celebration, quickly approved the suggestions, and the Hammerskin Nation was officially born. Even so, CASH voted to remain separate and operate independently for the time being.

When the fervor of the meeting cooled off a little, somebody suggested a beer run. Food and booze were running low. There was a grocery store next door, apparently an easy place to steal from. For the next hour or so, people ventured out in shifts, shoplifting food and alcohol and bringing it back to the apartment. Somebody stole a disposable camera and took pictures of people giving Nazi salutes, arms around each other, beers in hand. When it came my turn for the obligatory theft, I bought a bag of chips that was on sale. I couldn't risk getting caught stealing and have to explain to my parents what the hell I was doing way out in this neck of the woods, but I didn't want to come back empty-handed and look like a pussy either.

That night was the most alien and intense thing I'd ever experienced, and I was instantly hooked. I may not have come from a family down on its luck, and I hadn't been brought up to hate people different than me, but something about what I was learning made it seem like a truth that had for years been hidden from me. More than ever, I wanted to be part of this.

It was thrilling.

Grown up.

Real.

And it was black-and-white; no middle ground. I couldn't sit on my hands any longer. I had made my decision, and it was on this side of the fence where I landed firmly with both feet.

Looking at Scully's lily-white face, sensing his anxious urge to leave, I knew he was out. He wasn't a racist and avoided confrontation. I'd have to save the world without the help of my old friends. Or make new friends.

Here I was—all of fourteen years old, in at the ground level of something significant, with a real chance to make an impact, to demonstrate my courage. This was my family now.

Were black and Mexican people—excuse me, niggers and wetbacks—all that bad? Well, not by my previous limited experiences, but the skinheads saying this were older, wiser. They'd paid attention longer and understood the problems. They were the ones whose jobs were being taken over. And I wasn't all that down with minorities moving into my neighborhood. I could help keep Blue Island white. Italian. These older skins knew their shit. They were here to teach the rest of us, and I knew, with my ambition and talent, I would be able to help.

7

SUMMER OF HATE

BY THE END OF MY FRESHMAN YEAR of high school, I came and went from home as I damn well pleased. I snatched the keys and took my mom's car out for joyrides as if I owned it, unhindered by the fact that I was still too young to drive legally. I showed no respect in my speech or demeanor toward my parents, swearing at my father, walking out of the room whenever my mother tried to confront me about it.

They had stopped making any real efforts to interfere in my life after the last time my father had tried to smack the back of my head.

I'd come home drunk well after midnight one school night. My parents were perched at the front door waiting for me as I stumbled in.

My dad pounced on me before I was able to fully cross the threshold. "Where the hell have you been?"

I chuckled and retorted, "Where the hell have *you* been?"

My father's irritation quickly intensified to anger as my reaction to his scolding manifested as an apathetic fit of laughter. I brushed him off and made my way toward my bedroom. As I entered the kitchen, my father caught up to me and drew his hand back to slap my head. I may have been impaired at the time, slower in my reflexes, but I'd become conditioned to never let him fully out of my peripheral vision when he was incensed.

Christian Picciolini in his Nazi frat-boy dorm room, 1989

Before he could fully commit his swing, I turned and grabbed his arm mid-recoil and pinned the rest of his body hard against the refrigerator with my forearm. A ceramic vase with some acrylic flowers that rested atop the fridge came toppling down and crashed into pieces on the floor at the feet of my hysterical mother.

"Don't you ever fucking raise your hand to me again, or I'll hit you back ten times harder than you've ever hit me. And it won't be a little slap on the back of the head. Do you understand me?"

I pushed him away and continued staggering down the narrow hallway until I reached my bedroom, slamming the door hard. Immediately, I heard my mother wail in a way I'd never heard before. Now, what the hell is she screaming about? I thought.

"My God, Christian. Open the door!" My father stood outside my room, crying for me to unlock the door, pounding, trying frantically to turn the knob. My mom had unfortunately been just a step behind me as she laid her hand on the doorframe to stop me from slamming it. I'd crushed her middle finger in the doorjamb and she was bleeding profusely, dripping on the ceramic floor.

"That's what you get. Next time leave me the fuck alone," was all I said when I opened the door and realized what had happened. Needless to say, my words did not match how I felt. Inside, I was as torn up over it as her finger was.

My father wrapped my mom's bloody hand in a towel and drove her to the emergency room to get stitches.

The loud ruckus woke five-year-old Buddy. He started to cry as he wiped the sleep from his eyes and emerged from his room to see the anguish on my mom's face and the blood running down her arm.

I quickly let him into my bedroom, pulling him up into my arms to avoid the puddle of blood on the floor, and consoled him as we sat on my bed in the dark room. "Why is mommy crying, Buddy?" he sniffled.

"Because I made a mistake, Buddy." I couldn't lie to him. "She'll be okay. They'll be back soon."

"Okay." He rubbed his tired eyes. "Can I sleep in here with you tonight? I'm scared."

"Yeah, of course. Why are you scared, Buddy?" I wiped his tears with my thumb and held him close.

He was starting to doze off. "Because you smell like beer and you're fighting with Dad."

I kissed him on his forehead as his heavy eyelids shut.

I spent the rest of the night lying next to Buddy with a clenched chest and a lump in my throat, crying quietly inside and feeling deep regret for the pain I'd caused my mother. She never mentioned anything about the incident to me afterward, though I could sense how hurt she was by my actions. I never found the courage to apologize to her.

My father didn't stop giving me grief about it, but he never laid a hand on me again after that night.

Right before Marist let out for the summer, I let my parents know they'd better enroll me in a different school for my sophomore year. "I'm not going back to that mental prison."

"Christian," my mother scolded, "don't call such a nice Catholic school a prison. You did just fine there, and of course you'll go back."

"No way. They're brainwashed sheep. And you shouldn't even want me to go back. They wasted your precious work time calling you because I skipped school one day. Bullshit."

"It was silly for you to do that," my mother said. "But your father and I straightened it out for you, didn't we?"

"Straightened it out?" I said contemptuously. "What you did was lie."

"We protected you. What did you want us to do? Let them suspend our son?" my father said.

"The point is, you lied. Exactly like they do. Anyway, you should be glad I'm not going back. You won't have to make excuses for me anymore."

"Wait and see," my mother said, trying to gently embrace me. I snapped my body back, letting her know to keep her hands off me. She backed off, adding, "By the time summer is over, you will see it's the best school."

By now my parents knew I was becoming something else, no longer their innocent boy, but they assumed it was a teenage phase and didn't push back hard enough to realize it wasn't. Had they understood what I was up to, they would have seen that I'd substituted the attention I once longed for from them with something far more sinister.

My parents' two-flat building had a small private garden apartment that sat unrented, just accumulating boxes of clothing and old furniture. With some elbow grease and paint it would make a great little place to live. Without asking for permission, I commandeered the space. I gathered some free scrap material from the lumberyard and framed out a bedroom and living area.

Neither of my parents liked this idea, of course. My mother hated the notion I could now come and go as I pleased through a separate outside entrance. She wouldn't even be able to hear the door open or close, and I could have anybody I wanted down there. But for reasons that, in the wake of my bloody outburst, are easy to understand, neither of my parents stood up to me. They didn't have the courage anymore to go beyond trying to guilt me with a few forceful words.

The first thing I did after commandeering the basement was have Jessica Rimbaldi over. Tall, voluptuous Jessica with her long legs, dark eyes, and apple-red cheeks. Her full mouth and soft lips. My Nazi cheerleader girlfriend.

The first time we snuck into my basement apartment, the two of us laughed so hard we nearly wet our pants. The place wasn't finished yet, but we couldn't keep our hands off each other. Nearly every night and some days during school, we took advantage of the freedom that came with me having my own place.

Late one night while we were having sex, we heard my mother snooping by the front entrance. We must have been louder than we thought. I tried to pull my jeans on with one hand and shoved Jessica, as she was still getting dressed, out the window with the other, while my mom banged on the door like she was the damn FBI serving a felony warrant.

"Christian! Christian, open the door. What are you doing that takes you so long to answer me?"

The second Jessica's foot was outside, I shut the window and, zipping my pants, went to unlock the door. "What's your problem?" I snapped. "Can't you let me sleep?"

Suspecting something was amiss, my mother barged in and took her sweet time checking out my place. I wondered what the hell she would have done if Jessica had been in there.

By the time my mother was satisfied that her suspicions were unfounded and I had finished laying a guilt trip on her for waking me up and always being on my back, I went out to find Jessica. She was nowhere in sight. Obviously, she'd decided to walk the two miles home in the dark by herself.

Real chivalrous of me. Especially knowing that niggers were out there everywhere just looking for a beautiful white girl like her to rape. No fucking way. I'd kill someone if they so much as looked at her. They couldn't treat my girlfriend that way. Who did those animals think they were?

Nothing like that came to pass, but Jessica and I didn't last long after that night.

I worked quickly, motivated and driven by plans beyond what any other kid, even the High Street Boys, dared to concern themselves with.

Buddy, still a stout little guy full of wonder, would come down to look around. Just like I used to follow my grandfather around when he was building something in his workshop, my chunky little five-year-old brother watched me put up the walls in my new domain. He tried to help me paint. I let him hang out, like Nonno had let me when he was working. Buddy made a mess, but so what? It was how he'd learn. Watching his fifteen-year-old big brother would teach him all he needed to know.

Within two weeks, the place was ready. I used some of the old furniture my parents kept in storage and decorated my walls with neon beer signs and Nazi and Confederate flags for which I'd traded my old baseball card collection at the flea market.

"Can I live here with you, Buddy?" my little brother would ask. Of course he'd want to. I was his cool older brother. He'd want to do everything I did.

"I would love that, Buddy," I said, patting his little head, "But I'm sure Mom and Dad would really miss you if you didn't live with them."

"But I miss *you*," he said, his voice quivering. "Why did you have to move out?"

I was hit with a bitter wave of sadness brought about by the genuine innocence in his round brown eyes. Trying to respond without letting the lump forming in my throat get the best of me, I got on one knee and hugged him tightly. "Well, there are some things that I need to do, and sometimes it's best if I do them alone."

His bottom lip trembled. He fought back tears.

The lump in my throat was making it hard to talk. "Why don't you go and see what Mom made you for dinner?" He didn't move.

"Hey, you'll be right upstairs," I told him. "You can come down any time."

His big brown eyes lit up. "Really, Buddy?"

"Sure, Buddy." I patted his head. "We can even come up with a secret knock."

"Really?"

"You bet." I held my hand up for a high five. "Now get outta here," I said. "Go eat some pasta."

I shut the door behind him and leaned my back up against it as I wiped a tear from my eye. Then, taking a look around, I cleared my throat and grinned inside. I may not have had much, but I had my Nazi frat-boy dorm room.

I turned my attention fully to skinhead activities. I marched into the Blue Island post office, filled out an application, laid down twenty bucks, and took over a vacant slot next to the now-abandoned Romantic Violence post office box. I immediately began communicating through mail with other skinheads and white-power groups organizing across the country. There was no World Wide Web then, but the opportunity to build a real-life social network was there if you played it right and were willing to put in the work.

To be a leader, I knew I needed to show initiative, establish myself as dependable. Be innovative. I sorted the leaflets I'd been collecting from the older skinheads and began photocopying them at the local pharmacy, mailing them off to other skinheads with post office boxes halfway across the world. In the envelope I'd always include a handwritten note asking the recipient to pass along the literature to someone new after they'd read it, hoping to continue the chain indefinitely.

The first correspondence I sent out contained a copy of one of Clark's earliest writings. I clipped the article from one Tom Metzger's White Aryan Resistance newsletters:

> *How we cried out for help, for vengeance, for life. And yet our plea went unanswered for years, until it came—the plan of salvation, the hope of redemption; we became warrior skinheads!*

The literature that came in provided the addresses of other pro-white organizations, which I added to my mailing list. Ku Klux Klan. American Nazi Party. Aryan Nations. American Front. Church of the Creator. National Alliance.

As soon as I received a new flyer or newsletter, I reprinted copies and mailed them to other groups on my list, delivered them in bulk to other skinheads, or handed them out to local kids—skaters, punks, stoners, anyone who I thought might be convinced to get off their ass and do some good fighting for their future. I missed no opportunity to market the ideology of white supremacy. Now that Clark was doing hard time in prison and Carmine, Chase, and the rest of the original crew were avoiding the spotlight, I added my own words and contact information to anything I photocopied, personalizing the message about defending ourselves against inferior races as I spread information about rallies and meetings. I made sure my name and post office box address were on every piece of literature I sent out.

The summer of 1988 had proven to be a watershed moment, not only for me personally, but also for the burgeoning American neo-Nazi skinhead movement at large. It turned out I had begun to establish myself just as the storm clouds gathered. White-power groups began sprouting up like weeds in metropolitan areas across the country and, with the rapidly increasing numbers and the hottest summer temperatures recorded in over a century, utter pandemonium erupted.

American Front skins in Portland beat an Ethiopian immigrant student to death with a baseball bat. At least one Los Angeles skinhead was being tried for murder in another case involving a minority. The brand-new Tulsa, Oklahoma, Hammerskin crew that was particularly intent on causing as much violent mayhem as they could began taking great pleasure in targeting homeless blacks for random beatings, or "boot parties," as they called them. The detailed letters they'd sent me seemed to describe an endless supply of fodder for their vicious recreational activities. And, closer to home, six original CASH members, including Clark Martell, had been formally sentenced to lengthy terms in penitentiaries across the Midwest for charges including aggravated assault, criminal damage to property, and home invasion—a class X felony in Illinois.

While we may have publicly tried to wrap our politics in easier-to-swallow catchphrases like "white pride" and "pro-white" for the sake of positive marketing to the unwitting masses, our actions revealed that rather than peddling pride, we trafficked in hate. We fucking hated anyone who wasn't white and were willing to violently slaughter them.

Those ruthless few months in 1988 in which I came to call white supremacist skinhead culture my own went down in our circles as the "Summer of Hate."

Since the widely publicized Angie Streckler and *Kristallnacht* trials had resulted in a significant chunk of the CASH skins being imprisoned, the time was as good as any for me to make my mark. By now I'd become the only remaining active associate from the original CASH crew, and I began inheriting pieces of what Clark and Carmine and Chase had left behind. Best of all, I was still too young to be on the cops' radar. It wasn't long before any new recruits began to look to me for leadership and direction.

Becoming the de facto leader of the second wave of Chicago white-power skinheads took little serious effort. Blue Island was an easy place to recruit. Most kids and their families were barely making ends meet from one paycheck to the next, and they lived in a neighborhood that was rapidly deteriorating. Kids in Blue Island liked to let loose and blow off steam. Girls were equally willing to hang out. The guys were into music and could easily be persuaded to relate to the message I was pushing.

We needed to become magnetic. We partied, made sure we were seen, bowed to no authority. I pushed the militant skinhead lifestyle to the limits. Eager to sharpen my street-fighting skills at every opportunity, I picked fights in public with anyone I thought I could intimidate or outpunch. We were gentlemen thugs intent on having a good violent time while on duty protecting our race from our enemies. And our numbers grew rapidly.

One of my best recruiting scores was Al Kubiak.

Kubiak was a natural-born bruiser who loved to fight. He was solid and muscular, with a baby-faced grin, and he seemed to smile even wider when he was throwing punches. We hadn't liked each other much during my High Street days, when we'd been given to cursing at each other rather than sharing a beer or a kind word. He was a spoiled kid from the West Side of Blue Island, which made him an enemy of us East Siders.

We couldn't stand him and his group of friends, so if we caught them on our side of Western Avenue we'd try to chase them out.

But he was not keen on running away from confrontation. Kubiak always stood and fought while his friends ran, coming to blows, or backing down only if one of us happened to be carrying a baseball bat or a hockey stick. Every time he and I saw each other we called each other every foul name we could think of, but somehow we never threw fists. Then one day, he'd come to me after a party asking if he could become a skinhead, and suddenly we were on the same team.

If not for Kubiak's unwavering racist attitude and eagerness to punch people without provocation, I'd never have given him a second thought. But his skills could come in handy as I was growing our crew. He would be my extra muscle when I needed it. Our commitment to each other grew exponentially over the summer, cemented by our unspoken mutual desire to throw down with every wannabe gangbanger and Anti invading our territory. Kubiak thought nothing of walking up to non-whites and shoving them to provoke a fight. And when he did, I never hesitated to join in the fray.

Since the Jake Reilly romp in eighth grade, I'd taken to fighting with relative ease and comfort. My training came in the form of almost daily fistfights with anyone whom I felt threatened the safety of my neighborhood. Violence and dominance became pleasurable in a way that, when I remember it all these years later, makes me sick.

Sometimes Kubiak and I took on three, four, even five guys at once. The bigger, the better. They never saw it coming from such young guys. Our undying allegiance to each other and the element of surprise were definitely on our side. That's what best friends did together.

One testosterone-fueled weekend, Kubiak and I and couple of neighborhood guys jumped in a car and headed to the University of Illinois at Urbana–Champaign, a two-and-a-half-hour drive south of Blue Island, in central Illinois. An older brother of one of the other guys attended school there and invited us to come hang out and party for the night. The moment we arrived, aided by the fact that we'd been pounding beers the entire drive down, all hell broke loose.

The four of us arrived at the apartment complex where we were supposed to meet the brother and knocked on the door of the unit number we'd been given. It was loud and clear that a party was under way as the cacophony of music and conversations, even as we approached from down the hall, was deafening. No one answered when we knocked, so we let ourselves in.

As the four of us entered the overloaded apartment, the largest white human being I'd ever stood next to intercepted us immediately. This enormous, thick-necked, semi truck of a frat guy put his meat-hook hand on my shoulder and lurched me backward to align my face with his.

"If you jagoffs wanna come in, it's ten bucks apiece." His breath stung my eyes like rubbing alcohol and I pulled back.

"We're just looking for my brother. He told us to meet him here," one of our guys said. "His name is..."

"Hey, punk! Did you hear what I said?" the incredible white hulk cut in. "Twenty bucks."

"Twenty bucks?" Kubiak swiped the monster's hand off my shoulder. "You just said ten, King Kong."

He got in Kubiak's face. "Yeah, but I don't like you, so now it's thirty, sunshine."

"Yo, Gator, we got a problem here?" Another colossus from the party intervened and blocked our entry. This time it was a tall, lean, muscular black guy in a tank top and flip flops who was flanked by an equally large, muscled beast of a Samoan guy.

"No, fellas, we're all good here. I got this," I acquiesced as I reached toward my back pocket and threw a sideways look at Kubiak, who was thinking the same thing I was.

"Looks like I don't have a twenty," I said. "I only have five." I cracked Gator square in his jaw with a fistful of brass knuckles from my back pocket.

Kubiak grabbed the black guy and kicked him in the balls. He went down as Kubiak turned to slug the giant Samoan. He grabbed a beer bottle to smash across his face.

The other two skinheads with us started slugging anyone within arm's length. The stream of people coming at us seemed infinite.

Before we knew it, the four of us were punching, kicking, and smashing bottles over the heads of half of the University of Illinois football team's offensive line. These guys were big and strong, but none of them had any fighting experience like we did.

When the place began to look like a tornado had spun through it, with banged-up bodies and furniture strewn everywhere, drunken sorority girls shrieking, we bolted for the car.

On our way out of the complex, several of the neutral partygoers and a pizza delivery guy on a bicycle who had witnessed the action came up to pat us on the back and revel with us over our intense brawl. We'd trained ourselves to be so utterly, remorselessly violent that we started fighting even them and laid them out on the street.

We were banged up sufficiently, but we were the ones who could still walk out of that place on our own two feet.

Within minutes, the streets were swarming with dozens of police officers and a legion of campus security vehicles putting up roadblock checkpoints to try to track down the gruesome mob of thugs who were capable of inflicting that much damage and injury on their star football athletes. Lucky for us, they were searching for a large mob, not four high school-age dudes in a rusty Honda Accord. We were so busy re-enacting the brawl and laughing uncontrollably the whole drive home that we could hardly muster enough focus to get out of town.

The following Monday, a Blue Island police detective asked me to come down to the station to answer some questions about the incident. Apparently, the Illinois State Police had put out an APB for a dozen or more skinheads who'd brazenly assaulted and sent several University of Illinois football players to the hospital. Immediately all eyes fell on us, since we were the only skinhead crew in the state capable of such damage. Amused by the situation, I told the cops I had no idea who could have done such a thing. "After all, officer, I'm not even sixteen years old, and I don't have a driver's license or a car. How would I get down there?"

They couldn't prove it was us and dropped the investigation, but the guys and I laughed about it for weeks after that.

It didn't take many bruised and bloodied bodies for Kubiak and me to establish our notoriety as the two toughest motherfuckers around Blue Island. Every teenager in our neighborhood either looked up to us or feared us. Sometimes both. For the first time I felt completely in control of my own life. I'd yearned for so long to fit in with my peers, and now they'd begun to vie for my attention. The ones who had once ignored me, even those like Jake Reilly who had made fun of my foreign name, now seemed to respect me.

But beyond my own age group, I still wanted the respect of the older skinheads. I wrote to those doing time in prison. They'd eventually get out, and I counted on them standing at my side as an equal when that day came.

The main person to get to was still Clark. I wanted his official blessing. Nothing could top communication with him. Carmine gave me his address without hesitation, and I immediately began a regular correspondence with him in prison. I didn't expect him to answer, but I thought at least he'd start to appreciate the effort.

I added the numbers "14" and "88" right above my signature at the end of every letter I mailed out. The "14" represented our fourteen words, and "H" was the eighth letter of the alphabet, which, translated as "88," was secret code for "HH" or "Heil Hitler." Within a few weeks I was communicating not only directly with Clark, but also with dozens of other pro-white activists and prisoners across the country.

My parents eventually gave up their battle to send me back to Marist for my sophomore year. They still wouldn't let me go to Eisenhower, the public high school I could find myself tolerating, because my mother's experiences there had scarred her as a teen. Instead, they enrolled me in an experimental high school called Project Individual Education, or PIE, a small magnet school that took a sampling of kids from all three Blue Island–area public high schools. PIE was experimental in the sense that they tried to give students more educational freedom. Since it wasn't one of the primary public high schools in the area, my parents accepted that it was the next best thing to a private school. Buddy laughed at the funny name.

A few things put PIE above Marist in my book. Teachers seemed more relaxed, at least in theory. There was no more religion. And if you got good grades, you could "opt out" of going to certain classes. Not that that made any difference to me—I'd opt out of anything I damn well wanted, good grades or not. State law still gave my parents the authority to decide if or where I attended school, but they sure couldn't make me do anything I didn't want to once I was there.

The one truly great thing about PIE was its connection to Eisenhower. Since both schools belonged to the same district, it meant I would be allowed to play for Eisenhower's football team with Kubiak. Playing football on a real team was something I'd wanted to do since my High Street days. I loved being a gladiator out on that field, the promise of glory and of being a hero carried off the field on my teammates' shoulders that every game brought.

Despite our commitment to our racist doctrine, we managed to keep our white-power activity off the football field. In fact, my teammates—an equal mix of white, Latino, and black players—even nominated me as their team captain. Learning that news was the kind of heartbreaking moment that makes me wonder what could have been if I'd found help disengaging from the movement in time.

While I participated in football, I kept my racist sentiments to myself because I was determined to win above all else. As I learned to work with the black and Latino kids, even befriending a number of them, I reasoned that these particular "muds" weren't the same ones who were out there destroying our culture. These guys were okay. They were athletes whom I learned to trust, teammates with whom I'd shared moments of what felt like unparalleled greatness.

As soon as the games were over, Kubiak and I traded our football cleats for Doc Martens boots and were ready to ruthlessly stomp the enemies of our race.

8

YOUNG HATE MONGERS

I WROTE CLARK ABOUT OUR FREQUENT BRAWLS with the Antis and non-whites and updated him on the recruiting progress, knowing he'd be excited to hear I was carrying on his proud tradition. By this time, he was sending me three or four letters a week. I made sure the other skins knew I was in touch with him, to keep their spirits high, but I kept the content of his letters to myself.

To my dismay, as time passed, his packages arrived full of explicit pencil drawings of naked skinhead women attached to stories he had written that read like a Third Reich *Penthouse Forum*. It didn't seem right that he'd send me that weird shit, so I just tried to ignore it. Then whole notebooks full of erotic stories he'd written and illustrated started showing up. He became obsessed with a Chicago skinhead girl named Reina, whom he claimed to have knocked up before going to prison, and he had titled his pornographic Aryan love story *Right as Reina* in tribute. I'm not sure she knew about it or if she was really even pregnant with his child, but he epitomized her as the ultimate skinhead woman and wrote that she was the "goddess of all white women," while sketching her in intimate and provocative detail.

Clark also shared stories about how the prison guards treated him poorly and ranted about how he thought he was going mad.

The guards wouldn't let me out into the yard again today. The coons and queers get all the special privileges like extra juice and clean socks. I want clean socks too. I am not an animal. I am a political prisoner. God wants me to have clean socks and I'll have them if I want. I took a shit into my hands this morning and smeared my whole body with it so that I could look like a nigger and get an extra juice or package of bologna and some clean socks. But they didn't buy my ruse. The goons made it into my cell and bashed me before I was able to castrate myself with a sharpened salad tong I stole from the chow line yesterday. I'm writing you this letter from the psych ward. For God and Hitler and Reina! Hail Warrior Skinheads—C.M. 14/88.

Obviously, Clark's letters embarrassed me. There was no worse indictment of the white-power movement than where it had led my role model: into a prison's psych ward for smearing shit on himself and trying to cut off his own balls. But I couldn't face that truth yet.

I kept my thoughts private to protect his reputation—CASH's reputation. And what the hell, I rationalized, maybe it wasn't true insanity I was seeing. Maybe it was just desperation from being locked up. He was the first person—the Aryan Johnny Appleseed—to bring the white-power skinhead lifestyle to America, and people still trembled when they heard his name. Jewish watchdog organizations like the Anti-Defamation League always reported he was a top neo-Nazi sociopath, "one of the most terrifying men in America," and that reputation had to be tough, a burden to always have to live up to. The stuff of heroes and revolutionaries. I ended up burning the notebooks and letters he sent to me.

In November of my sophomore year, television talk show host Geraldo Rivera invited three skinheads, as well as John Metzger—the leader of the White Aryan Resistance's Aryan Youth Movement—to appear on his show for an episode called "Young Hate Mongers." To up his ratings, he also invited Roy Innis, a race-baiting civil rights activist who chaired the Congress of Racial Equality—CORE—and some "we are God's chosen people" Jew rabbi.

Not long into the interview Metzger called Innis an "Uncle Tom" for helping push the U.S. government's multiracial agenda and also criticized him for not admitting that blacks were a detriment to civilized white culture. In response, Innis jumped out of his chair and began choking Metzger on stage. Metzger defended himself, Geraldo got back on stage to intervene, and as all hell broke loose a skinhead in the crowd threw a chair in his general direction, catching him square in the face and busting Geraldo's nose wide open. The braver people in the audience streamed up on stage and joined in the melee; others in the audience acted like lunatics, scared to death, not knowing what to do as they huddled in a back corner of the studio.

This made national news on every television network, every newspaper, magazine, and radio station. Pundits and shock jocks rehashed the clip over and over again. And we celebrated. Far from proving we were barbarians like the media typically portrayed us, the interview showed three clean-cut, well-dressed, articulate if woefully misinformed neo-Nazi skinheads stating our purpose, defending our ideals. The leftist activist whom we at the time thought of as "the Big Ape" proved to be the instigator. The rabbi was an afterthought.

Still, the newspapers focused mainly on the "racist violence." Soon after, media reports began cropping up accusing white-power skinheads of attacking people in malls, pulling race-mixing couples out of their cars and beating them. The press called us out for the animals we were with headlines containing words like "Amoral thugs," "Outlaws," "Hatemongers," "Cockroaches." The media coverage incensed me. Had they not witnessed the literal physical defense of our philosophy? My frustration with the reporting inspired me even more. The lies that spewed seemed further evidence that our theories of Jewish control and censorship in the media were on the right track. I was beginning to feel that I was a part of something far bigger than Blue Island where it began, bigger than Chicago, even Illinois. Our American skinhead numbers were growing rapidly, and we were making ourselves known worldwide.

Kubiak thought it was time to be armed. Nothing fancy. He handed me a rusty semiautomatic .25-caliber pistol that he had stolen from his uncle.

The gun didn't weigh much, but it was heavy in my hand, and it made my heart beat faster. Power surged through my fingertips, tightening around the pearly grip. I straightened my arm, held it out, felt the energy of the weapon join with my own.

"Holy shit," I said.

Kubiak shrugged. "I'm not sure it works, but what the hell, you pull it on anyone, they won't know. I guarantee they'll back down."

I tucked it in my waistband where nobody could see it and walked home, conscious of the metal against my skin with every step.

I let myself into my basement flat and sat down on my bed. I took the gun out, stuck it back in my waistband and drew it over and over, practicing so I could draw quickly when the time came. I aimed it. I watched myself in the mirror.

I heard my mother shuffling outside the door, calling for me—spying on me again. I pointed my gun at the door, imagining what my mother would do if she opened it and met the barrel of my gun. "I'm sleeping. Leave me alone," I answered.

With everything that was happening on a national level, I knew I had to stay well informed. So I turned to *The Turner Diaries*, the novel that

Clark had given me for an education on survival. Clark called it "the Bible of the white revolution." William Pierce, a visionary, the leader of the white supremacist group National Alliance, wrote it under the pen name Andrew MacDonald in 1978. The book was written in journal form and chronicles Earl Turner's part in the violent overthrow of the U.S. government and the societal cleansing of all Jews and non-whites. It was his prophecy about what would happen in the not-too-distant future if white people didn't wake up now and take action.

I read the captivating account of our chilling future in less than six hours, and to say it inspired me would be an understatement. It incited me to the point that I wanted to mimic the heroic protagonist revolutionary in every action he took.

I would be Earl Turner, ready to take on my own government through violent means if that's what it took to set the world straight and protect what I loved.

First, though, I had a minor annoyance to deal with at PIE: a gangbanger named Damarcus, a black student who knew to stand his ground. Walking down the hallway one day he had the balls to deliberately step in my way and bump me. I struck first, landed a blow that split the bridge of his nose and grappled him into a headlock, ramming his head into the lockers before he knew what hit him. Dragging him bleeding from one side of the hallway to the other, I smashed his face against the steel doors before the gym teacher and the janitor got between us and broke it up. Some other teachers held me back and marched me to the principal's office.

It was the end of my time at PIE. A week after I got expelled, I returned and spray-painted "Niggers Go Home" in two-foot-high white letters across the school's front doors in case any of the black kids hadn't gotten the point when Damarcus got banged up.

The cops knew it was me. Of course it was. Everybody knew it. But they were unnerved by me at this point and were certain that targeting me would cause a backlash from my crew, since I'd managed to recruit more than a half dozen students during my brief time at PIE. Uneasy about the influence I'd amassed and certain there wasn't a thing they could do without hard evidence, they let it die. There was no school left for me at this point but the Blue Island public school system, which broke my mother's heart. She wanted me to be a doctor, and now I'd be in the horrible school she'd attended as a young, bullied sixteen-year-old immigrant. In truth, it may have made no difference in my life where I went at that point. I had more critical priorities on my mind. White revolution was my primary course of study.

9

HEAR THE CALL

ONE PIVOTAL THING HAPPENED during my time at Eisenhower. I met Tracy Connelly and entered the portal to an entirely new level of violence. But this time the perceived enemy was white like me.

Tracy was a year older than me. Pretty and unabashedly outspoken, she smoked and drank, and her innocence had vanished like aerosol hair spray long before we'd met. Abrasive as they come, she lived with her single mom, whom she tormented more than I did my parents, which was quite a feat.

She didn't go to Eisenhower, and she lived in Beverly, a predominantly Irish South Side neighborhood in the southwest corner of Chicago next to Blue Island. Kids from Beverly and kids from Blue Island lived only blocks apart but were more likely to spit or throw beer bottles at each other than trade pleasantries when our paths crossed. Few friendships existed between the two groups, and while it wasn't exactly a Romeo and Juliet situation if people from the different neighborhoods dated, there was an unspoken rule against it that few ignored.

What did I care? There sure as hell was no way anybody would tell me or Tracy who we could and could not mess around with.

Not long after Tracy and I began dating, her mother had her

committed to an alcoholism treatment facility for a week after she got wasted and hurled a cordless phone at her mother's head. Tracy gave her mother all sorts of stress. Not to mention stitches.

When Tracy got out of rehab, I made off with my parents' car and drove over to her house to make up for lost time. I'd gotten to be a decent driver over the last few months, despite still not being old enough to have my driver's license.

Taking the car after my parents went to sleep had become easier after the first few times. I'd swiped the keys from my dad's coat and made copies at the hardware store. Buddy had even seen me pulling into the driveway very early one morning while he was watching Saturday morning cartoons, but only smiled at me from the window and never squealed. My parents never questioned me about taking the car. I'm sure they suspected it but were too afraid to confront me, knowing that I'd take the argument far beyond just taking the car and do something really reckless to piss them off even more. In fact, ever since I'd threatened my dad with physical violence the last time he tried to punish me, he hardly spoke to me anymore.

There Tracy and I were, sitting on her front steps making out the night she got out of alcohol rehab, not doing a damn thing to piss anybody off, when six drunken Irish Beverly Boys—a bunch of guys not unlike the High Street Boys, but prone to fighting—settled themselves across the street in an open field, passing around a flask of liquor. Soon they started acting tough and calling out to Tracy: "Hey, Tracy, got a phone handy? Your mom called, said she wants it back." They howled with laughter.

"Why didn't you pick up the telephone when I called, Tracy? Guess you couldn't hear it since it's all busted up."

I rose. Tracy took my hand, trying to pull me back down. "There's six of them," she cautioned. "And they're trashed."

She was right, but on the other hand, this was my girl, and I wasn't about to listen to this crap from a pack of drunken micks.

I pulled my hand away. "They're getting on my goddamn nerves."

Fists clenched, I walked off into the black night, determined to shut them up. The second I reached them, without saying a word, I pulled my arm back and swung at the first human shadow I saw. They were on me faster than skate punks on speed, coming at me from all sides. One tried to throw me to the ground, but the others were too close and broke my fall. I swung with a roundhouse punch, quickly calculating the odds were good that with this many people on me, my blow would land on someone. My fist collided with someone's face, and I was rewarded by the familiar warmth of fresh blood. I took a sharp blow from a metal pipe to the gut. Pissed at the gall, I drove my head hard up into someone's chin, knocking him down. He grabbed at the darkness as he fell, taking someone with him. I took a barrage of quick, steady blows to my head, shoulders, kidney. One punch landed squarely in my abdomen and knocked the wind out of me. I doubled over.

"Had enough?" someone huffed.

Tracy was watching. I'd fight until I was unconscious. I sucked in my breath, sprung back up and landed a punch solidly on someone's jaw. I watched him reel back. I kept throwing rapid punches and connecting. My fists were throbbing. Seconds seemed like hours.

"Fellas. Give it up," someone from the Beverly group yelled. "He's fucking nuts. He ain't worth our time."

They retreated into the blackness. Tracy, beside me now, grabbed my arm and held her body against mine. I was out of breath.

"Let them go," she said. "They quit. Not you."

"Tell her you're sorry," I bellowed after them.

"Over your mother's dead dago body," someone echoed from the ether.

Fighting words. "Come back and say that to my face, you fucking Irish faggot," I hollered.

They disappeared across the prairie. Drama over.

For the night.

But the gauntlet had been thrown and the call to war issued. They knew it. I knew it. Tracy knew it.

By morning, the news that six Beverly Boys had jumped me and couldn't take me down had spread all over Blue Island and Beverly.

My Blue Island friends were out for blood. "Six of them attacked one of us? They're fucking dead," became a rallying cry.

The Beverly crew prepared for battle.

Never mind we were all white. Race didn't matter. This was about turf. Respect. And a statement that when someone messed with one of our own, there would be a war.

A war.

I'd started a fucking war.

Once again I had slotted myself perfectly into the role of protagonist—or antagonist, depending on whom you were talking to. Pitting my tribe against the other. The thrill of combat was supreme. Commanding a legion of soldiers, a group intent on achieving a singular goal, felt natural to me. It didn't matter if the opposition involved another sports team, our political enemies, or a rival neighborhood. My world was one in which belonging and identity hinged on taking sides, and I needed to lead the one that won.

10

WHITE PRIDE

THE BLUE ISLAND CREW—THE REMAINING CASH skinheads, Kubiak, and the two dozen or so teenagers I'd recruited in the time since Clark had gone to prison—and the Beverly Boys waged an all-out war against each other for the rest of my sophomore year in high school. For some reason, it didn't occur to us that we had more in common than not. Like my skinhead pals, the Beverly kids were racist. Their Irish families—made up mostly of cops, firefighters, and city workers—had kept Beverly fairly white and proudly proclaimed it was one of the last white bastions in the city of Chicago. Their politically connected parents had made sure of that. Most of the Beverly crowd also had short-cropped hair and had begun sporting skinhead attire: combat boots and bomber jackets.

But it didn't matter. Both of our groups needed a conduit for our aggressive agendas. And, because of that, we found it easy to hate each other's guts.

One night a bunch of us chased Rooney, an obnoxiously ballsy kid from the Beverly group, down an alley and cornered him next to a pickup truck loaded full of construction debris. As he evaded my grasp and tried to run, I grabbed a brick from the truck bed and hurled it at him, striking him square in the base of the neck from about ten yards away. From

Christian Picciolini cutting a new recruit's hair, 1989

that night on, the Beverly guys referred to me as "Brickolini." The Blue Island–Beverly war didn't play directly into my plans to save the white race, but because of it, my prominence as a leader, as someone capable of controlling the activities of a large area and everyone in it, had become certain.

One Saturday night, in our general fuck-the-world-and-everybody-in-it frame of mind, my skinhead friends and I headed over to initiate one of our frequent sneak attacks on the Beverly Boys. We were in war mode and didn't need a reason to attack them on any night in particular. That they existed on the other side of whatever imaginary line we'd created was all the provocation we needed.

When we busted into the garage housing their little get-together, looking to fight, one of their guys held out a beer instead. He was half loaded already, standing in the shadow of a Confederate flag dangling from the ceiling.

"What the fuck, Brickolini," he said. "It's been a year already. Ain't you sick of fighting us yet? Have a beer and relax."

Stunned silence from both camps.

People looked at me for direction.

I shrugged.

What the hell? The battle was over.

I reached for the beer and cracked it open. "By the way, that's not my name. You can call me Chris."

Instantly, we forgot all about being enemies, and for the next several years there was an unprecedented bond between the skins in Blue Island and the racist Beverly crew, and from then on we would work to spread hate together.

I'd changed in the few years since I'd found my home with the High Street Boys, and while those years were mostly carefree and innocent, the time with the Beverly Boys was marked by drunken get-togethers and constant street fighting. We got together every night at the nearby Mount Hope Cemetery, drinking cheap beer the Beverly crew had stolen from their alcoholic Irish fathers. With booze in hand, we climbed through a hole in the fence next to the train tracks that ran through Beverly and Blue Island to get into the graveyard. We settled in near the mausoleums and sat back to get blitzed.

We talked racist shit, and they ate it up. I handed out cassette copies of Skrewdriver records and passed along pointers on recruiting kids to join the movement. An easy thing to accomplish. It didn't even matter if they wanted to shave their heads and wear boots—though they usually did; all that mattered was whether they were willing to fight alongside us.

It took little skill to spot a teenager with a shitty home life. Somebody without many friends, looking confused or lonely, angry or broke. We would strike up a conversation, find out what they were feeling bad about, and move in with the pitch. "Man, I know exactly how that is. If your dad hadn't lost his job, it wouldn't be like that. But the minorities get all the jobs, catch all the breaks. They move into our neighborhoods and start getting handouts funded by us. Our parents work hard every day to put food on the table while the lazy blacks and Mexicans are cashing welfare checks in their sleep."

Before I knew it, there were a half dozen newly shaved heads coming to our weekly meetings, looking for something to belong to. To be somebody. We gave their lonely, shitty lives purpose. They were just like me two years earlier when I'd been vying for Clark's and Carmine's attention.

Soon enough, there were dozens of kids falling all over themselves helping me make copies of literature at the post office, and more cassette tapes to hand out, spreading the white-power gospel.

The sudden control was intoxicating.

I was able to host a recruitment rally in a church once because I'd homed in on Tim Morrison, a fresh-cut skinhead wannabe whose Lutheran minister father had mentally abused him as a child. I heartlessly exploited his hatred for his dad, convincing him to steal the keys and letting me hold the meeting there without his father's knowledge.

Almost twenty new kids attended that night. I dressed like a Nazi commander in a light brown military button-up shirt I'd purchased at a thrift store for a dollar and to which I'd attached a homemade swastika armband. Flanked by Nazi battle flags that I'd hung on either side of the altar, I told those who came that my vision was to see filthy race traitors hanging from every light pole up and down Western Avenue from Blue Island to Beverly. My words echoed in the vastness of the hall.

The more seasoned soldiers like Kubiak seated in the church gallery stood up and threw out their arms in glorious salute; the newcomers imitated. Kubiak pushed aside the Bibles stacked at the ends of the pews to make room for more recruits. From the pulpit I spat words of hatred, imitating for my audience those I'd seen in my role before me. "The revolution is coming and without forcing change now, future generations of white kids will not live in a free and just society. The white-power movement is about standing up to those who want to take our freedom away from us, before it's too late.

"Look at what's happening in your schools. Black kids are favored. They can wear racist Malcolm X T-shirts and celebrate criminals like Martin Luther King. Teachers encourage them to embrace their black heritage and openly teach about black pride.

"What about white pride? What's wrong with that? Speak up and you're told to shut up. Wear a proud symbol of the white race like the swastika, and you're branded a hatemonger and ostracized. Ask me. I'm living proof of that.

"I'm telling you that we can change that. We *must* change it or face extinction as a proud people. I will not stand to see our great European heritage wiped out and replaced by subhuman scum who contribute nothing to our world. There is a simple solution. A final solution. We must secure the existence of our people and a future for white children!"

The crowd rose to their feet and repeated the fourteen words. Proper "heil Hitler" salutes pierced the air.

The day after the meeting, someone who'd attended—perhaps an informant planted by the cops, who had to be well acquainted with my exploding group—told the media about the gathering and what I'd said. A local newspaper published the story and interviewed my high school principal, staff, and several of my classmates, all grappling with the inconsistencies of my message. Cops and teachers and the principal all commented on how troubled I must be to say what I did. The increased exposure kept some of the new kids away and made it hard to recruit for a while. The church also got a prominent mention in the article, and my friend's abusive dad had to resign. At least it wasn't a total bust.

By now, I'd made the call to retire the CASH moniker and adopt the Hammerskin brand, the name established by the Dallas skinhead crew at that cramped meeting in the Naperville apartment a few years earlier. We had expanded our group significantly, and falling under the flag of a growing international network of skinhead cells made sense. But only the name had changed. I had no intention of answering to anyone else.

As we were becoming nationally recognized, our neighborhood of

Blue Island was changing, and in our deranged logic it seemed our enemies were bringing the looming race war to us.

Restless, Kubiak and I were ever alert for a chance to clamp down and kick some ass. And now the Beverly kids and several dozen new recruits from around Chicago were right there beside us to help, though they had their hands full cleaning up their own neighborhoods.

We beat the piss out of anyone who didn't look like us whenever we got the chance. One of the nastiest fights began in a McDonald's restaurant on Western Avenue and 119th Street—the crossroads that separated Blue Island from Beverly and the Chicago city limits. A few Beverly kids and I had stopped in for something to eat late one night after drinking in the cemetery, and we ran into four belligerent black teenagers standing in line.

"Well, if it ain't a bunch of fucking monkeys. You guys escape from the zoo?" My friends and I loudly expressed that we were the only people with a right to be there. We circled the muds, staring them down. They quickly realized they were outnumbered and scurried out.

With a roar, we charged out of the restaurant after the four black teens. Fifty yards into the chase, one of them turned mid-sprint, pointed a pistol, and opened fire on us.

Three rapid shots whizzed past our heads as the smell of spent gunpowder trails filled our nostrils. Then the pistol jammed.

We didn't break stride. Rather than scaring us off, the gunshots incited us. "These worthless animals are trying to kill us in our own neighborhood," I said.

The one who'd taken the shots at us dropped the faulty gun. Moving through the darkness faster than bullets, we caught up with him, slammed him to the ground. We kicked him in the ribs, the back, the head, steel toes cutting through his skin.

We were relentless. He was no longer able to defend himself; the jolts to his body from our heavy boots sent spasms through the motionless bag of broken bones.

We thought the blood that stained the pavement served as a testament to our cause, that we had honored the fourteen words.

Night surrounded us, and the boy's white teeth were now stained red. These gangbangers from the South Side of Chicago may have been tough, raised by hardened parents who'd lived through the civil rights riots of the sixties, but they weren't fighting for a purpose or prepared for a race war.

As I stood over the limp and brutalized body, the boy's frightened, swollen eyes showed a sliver of life and connected with mine. I realized then that he couldn't have been much older than twelve or thirteen, and I thought of my six-year-old brother. The bloated, bloodshot eyes that gazed up at me from the ground pleaded for his life and penetrated my soul.

Sirens cut through the night and broke my daze. When the cops were around the corner, the rest of the guys stopped kicking. We got away, and for the first time the violence of a fight had left me feeling somber and dejected.

The remaining months of 1989 were full of skinhead and white supremacist rallies in Indiana, Wisconsin, and Michigan. No longer a quiet observer, I spoke my mind—that is, the caustic groupthink that I'd now spent two years filling my mind with. "Fourteen words," I'd shout from the front of the room as I greeted everyone with a stiff-armed salute. I was unafraid to voice the rhetoric I knew by heart, high on the respect and attention it got me. I may not have been the oldest, being just sixteen, but I was often among the most dedicated, respected, and tenacious.

Life was a constant redline. The faster I went, the further in my rearview mirror lay comfort. From time to time, I may have felt guilty for my actions and pondered whether all the white supremacist stuff I was feeding these kids was right. It didn't always go down so easily for me—the anxiety from the constant violence that existed twenty-four hours a day, the hateful ideology I programmed myself with to override the old-world values I'd been raised on. I'd resolved to bury those doubts deep down where they couldn't be misinterpreted as any signs of weakness, and it would turn out that I had buried them so deep it would take a virtual exorcism to uncover them.

One night I caught my mother going through my things in my basement apartment.

"What the hell?" I yelled, grabbing the shirt she had in her hand. "This is my room. My stuff. You have no right to be in here."

She didn't correct me. Instead she trembled, looking helplessly at the swastika T-shirt I'd snatched back from her. "Why, Christian?" she cried. "We didn't raise you to be this. This Nazi nonsense. This Hitler. All the killing. He was an evil man. Why don't you pick an Italian for a hero? Anyone would be better. Even Al Capone."

Her ignorance astounded me.

"Stay out of here," I ordered.

She backed out, momentarily cowering. To reassert her authority, she brought my brother into it, knowing Buddy was the only family member I felt tenderness for. "Alex misses his big brother. Maybe you can stay home more and play with Buddy."

Once she was beyond the threshold, I slammed the door in her face and leaned my back up against it. Tired, I slumped over and rested my head in my hands. The rapid knocks coming from the other side of the door infuriated me, and I threw it open, shouting, "Leave me the fuck alone and stay the hell out of here!"

It was little Buddy. He began to sob and backed away from me. I'd frightened him.

"No, no! I'm sorry, Buddy. I thought it was—never mind—I didn't mean that." I reached out to comfort him, but he ran away bawling.

My desperate mother had figured out how to get through. If only I'd been brave enough to let the realizations the world was beginning to bring before me change my course.

11

ARMED AND DANGEROUS

I STARTED MY JUNIOR YEAR back at Eisenhower in Blue Island. Known throughout the school as a hardcore racist and bruiser not to be messed with, I was left alone by most people. Teachers knew I was intelligent. When I actually went to class, I'd ace their stupid honors tests despite my lack of interest. But they didn't want me in their classrooms anymore. The football coaches who'd once clamored for me cut their losses and avoided me. Perhaps I was a star athlete with fire in my eyes, but now more importantly I was a liability.

I lasted at Eisenhower until November of my junior year. I'd missed twenty-four school days in the first three months of school, which was almost half of my total class time. Even when I was there, I cut out during lunch period to screw around with whatever girl I was seeing at the time or check the post office box and answer some of the dozens of pieces of correspondence I received every week. The dean called my parents and told them he couldn't let me continue there because of my truancy. They did what they knew best, tucked their tails and enrolled me in Brother Rice High School, another private Catholic school in the city. I couldn't believe it.

It wouldn't take long before I stopped going to class there and was expelled.

Christian Picciolini and crew, 1990

One night one of the Beverly guys and I were in a local record shop trying to convince the purchasing manager to start selling Skrewdriver records, when we spotted a couple of skinhead-looking kids we'd never seen before, which made it a safe bet they were Antis. One was wearing an oxblood-colored bomber jacket. "That's a cool bomber," I said to my friend. "It'd look good on me. That Anti has no right to wear it."

We left the store and got into the beater car we'd come in, so rusted that both bumpers had fallen off long ago, and pulled up beside the entrance waiting for the two guys to emerge. When they were close to our car and I was sure no one was watching, I swung the door open and confronted the kid with the jacket, thrusting my broken .25 semi-auto into his ribs.

"Give me the jacket, motherfucker." I directed his attention to the gun to emphasize my point.

"Don't give him shit!" his wiseass partner said, not noticing the weapon that was shoved in his friend's gut. He walked around to the back of the car to look for the license plate, then dashed to the front of the car, his cocky expression turning pale when he saw there wasn't one in either spot and I was holding a pistol.

I raised the gun and pressed it under the kid's chin. "Your jacket. Now!"

He tore it off, held it out in his trembling hands.

"Do you know who I am?" He nodded his head to indicate he did. "Good. Then you also know that if you say anything to the cops, I'll find you and fucking kill you."

I backed into the car and we tore out of the parking lot.

"Jesus Christ," the Beverly kid said, cringing. "That's armed fucking robbery. And that kid knows who you are!"

"He won't say shit." I checked the side mirror for a sign of the cops. "Let's get off the main streets."

We wove in and out of side roads all the way home. Halfway across town, I took my jacket off at a stoplight and tried the new one on. Too damn small. Son of a bitch! I searched the pockets and felt some paper. After pulling it out, I instantly recognized it as one of my flyers. I'd just managed to strong-arm one of my own recruits.

Not long after I was expelled from Brother Rice for missing classes and all the subsequent detentions I was supposed to serve to make up for them, my parents crawled back to Eisenhower and begged them to let me in so I could stay on track to graduate. Reluctantly and with stipulations, the school agreed, my mother and father no doubt full of promises that this time would be different. Which of course it wouldn't be.

Indifferent to the whole situation, I somehow managed to complete the rest of my junior year at Eisenhower without significant incident, mainly because I was under constant surveillance by an off-duty police sergeant the principal hired specifically to monitor me during school hours. I couldn't make a move without that cop on my tail.

My parents took an arm's-length approach to my problems, and after my frequent violent outbursts, I couldn't blame them. I depended on them for basic needs like food and shelter, but otherwise we kept our distance. They'd been so busy trying to manage their business and taking on second and third jobs to support their impersonation of a middle-class life, in some way they'd forgotten that anything outside of that pursuit existed. I resented them for that.

When she was home, my mother occasionally hassled me about my friends and activities. My dad couldn't get it through his head that I was long beyond his control. Buddy had forgiven me for yelling at him, but I was becoming increasingly distant and quiet.

During the summer break between my junior and senior year, with Kubiak as my right-hand partner in crime and most of the Blue Island and Beverly kids on my side, there was nothing I felt I couldn't do. Beyond my local community, my notoriety around Chicago also began to grow. All the respect and acceptance I'd ever longed for when I was invisible as a child was now mine.

Everybody knew my name, wanted to hang out with me, or was scared shitless of me. I needed to do no more than suggest something, and it happened.

Antis bugged me, so we locked horns with them every time we got a chance. Things heated up to the point that a huge brawl with them was all anyone talked about anymore. We all knew it was coming. A date finally emerged without any specific planning. Just one of those things. One person told someone to "go fuck yourself." Another said something else in return. Tempers flared. Somebody challenged somebody, and a date was set.

The Beverly Boys heard what was going on and pledged their support. To my surprise, so did every other white clique around town, including most of the jocks, metal heads, and stoners from Blue Island—people who knew me and what I was about, but whose names I could never remember. Word about the rumble spread fast and the Beverly prairie was chosen as the battlefield.

Night of the fight, our group showed up first, with an endless row of cars already lined up when another twenty or so cars full of supporters pulled up. Kids came from everywhere, including neighboring towns and the city, to back us up.

Then came the Antis. Dozens of them.

Altogether there were more than a hundred kids in the prairie that night ready to brawl.

The Antis initiated the action and jumped out from behind buildings, pumped, thinking they were going to ambush us. But they didn't take more than a few steps before they realized just how many people had come out to support us. Our cause. Our beliefs.

The Antis backpedaled slowly, and then as they saw us moving in, they broke into a retreating sprint.

We tore off after them, shouting obscenities, swinging sawn mop handles, padlocks, chains wrapped around clenched knuckles, baseball bats cutting through the air.

But there weren't as many of them as there were of us, so they had an advantage in terms of mobility. The sheer number of us slowed us down as we got in each other's way, shoving to be the first to draw blood.

They outran us.

Disheartened that our moment to destroy the enemy had come and gone without a single punch being thrown, we retreated back to the prairie to celebrate and get drunk. While we proclaimed victory and laughed about their cowardice, a few Antis snuck back to the prairie and attacked our cars, throwing bricks, kicking in fenders, trying to smash headlights and windshields with their boots, ripping off car antennae, slashing tires, any meaningless thing that would give them bragging rights.

But we were on our feet when we heard the shattering glass and gave chase quickly.

Again, they outran us.

We settled in with our beer, proclaiming ourselves the true victors, but knowing full well none of us could claim that in this non-fight, especially not us with the torn-up cars. "They're nothing more than race-traitor faggots," a cute blond cheerleader said.

"Damn right," we agreed, popping open more cans of beer and toasting our victory.

"Heil Hitler," another stranger shouted.

"Fucking A," I replied. "Heil Hitler." The sign of unity from people that I didn't even know fed my ego, notwithstanding the result of the confrontation. I feasted on the popularity.

All types of white youth—jocks, stoners, skaters, bookworms, cheerleaders, preps, you name it—began to look up to me, emulate me. And with their admiration, I would feel myself stuffing any doubts about our purpose deeper. To this day it is that inaction toward my ambivalence that I regret the most.

The recruitment pool was overflowing, and we spent the rest of the summer drinking like thirsty Vikings and listening to blaring white-power music with fresh faces, going to local rallies and battling a brand-new wave of anti-racists called SHARPs—Skinheads Against Racial Prejudice.

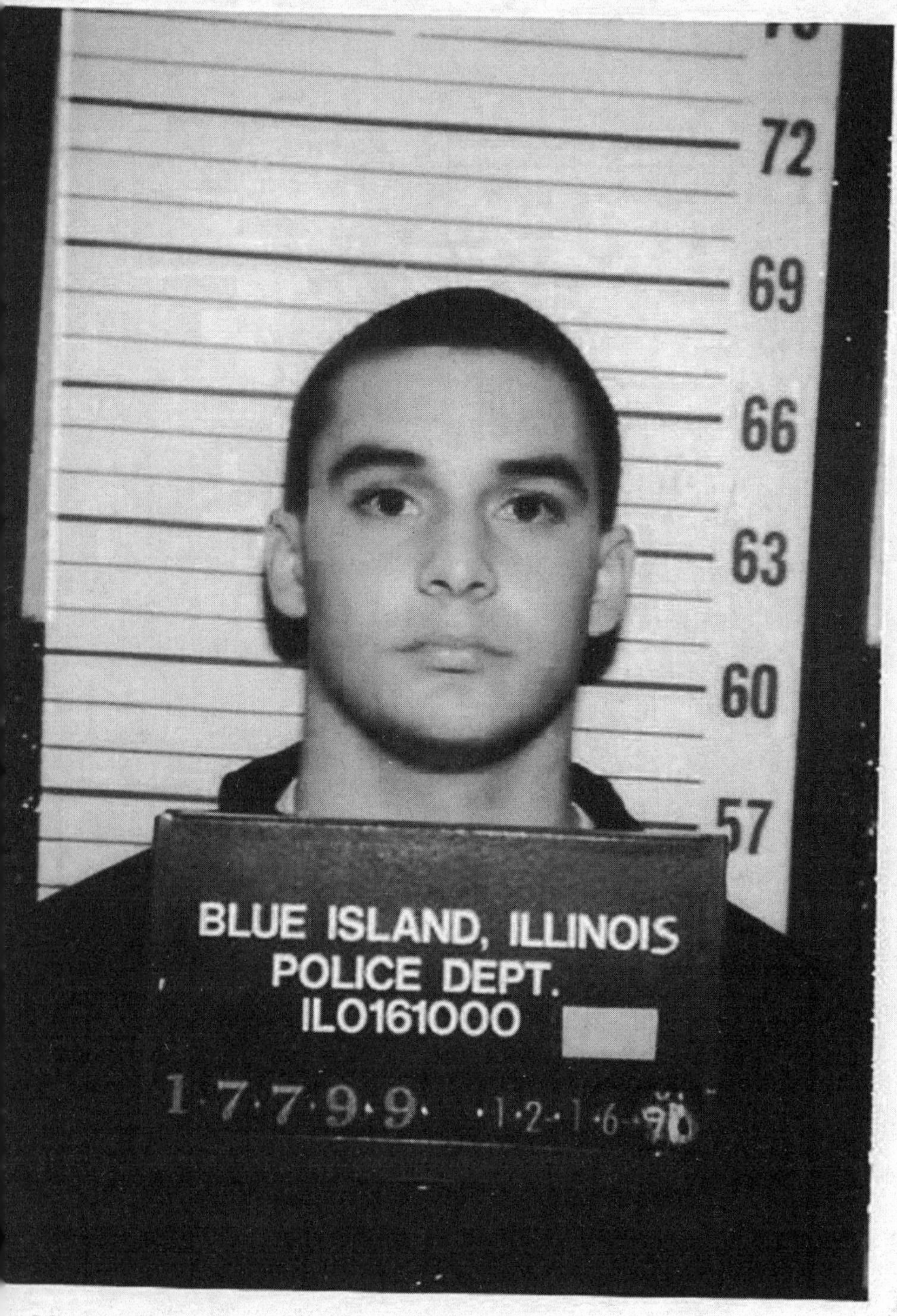
72
69
66
63
60
57
BLUE ISLAND, ILLINOIS
POLICE DEPT.
IL0161000
17799

, Chris M

12

W.A.Y.

IN LATE 1990, when September and my senior year rolled around, I was impatient to start high school so I could get it over with once and for all. It was the last year I'd be subjected to know-nothing teachers and under the thumb of a family who refused to support my vital mission.

The new Eisenhower principal warned me shortly before classes started that even a small disruption would get me kicked out permanently, so I did try toning down my rhetoric during school at first for the sake of graduating. But despite my effort to skate through my last year of high school, there was no realistic chance I would fit in. It was way too late for that. I had serious goals that I wanted to achieve, and I'd outgrown school and everyone in it. Not only did I not belong there, nobody wanted me around. Administrators feared I'd cause a race riot in an already volatile racially mixed environment. Teachers distrusted me. They worried I'd disrupt their classes and make it hard for other students to learn. To make it all worse, it seemed obvious to me they favored blacks over whites, giving them better grades for less work, letting them get away with shit the white kids never got away with, like swearing in class and showing up late after the bell. They never even confronted the Mexican students because the language barrier was too great. And to top it off, the new Eisenhower

Christian Picciolini, Blue Island Police Department mugshot, 1990

principal—a black woman—thought she could keep my crew and me in check.

It all came to a head when a black student and I got into a fierce verbal argument in art class when he refused to move away from the door as I tried to enter the classroom. Of course, the queer art teacher assumed it was my fault and sent *me* to the office to be reprimanded, but not the other kid. I sat there waiting outside the principal's door, stewing for a few minutes, before coming to my senses.

Incensed, I eventually pushed back my chair outside the office, knocking it to the floor with a loud bang, and I tore up two flights of stairs, where I threw open the heavy door to the art room with a wall-shaking rattle. As every wide-eyed, startled face in the room turned to make sense of the sudden commotion, I flew across the classroom so fast my Docs hardly hit the floor before I tackled the arrogant bastard who was perched triumphantly on his tall art stool.

"I write the rules here, you fucking nigger," I roared, dragging him to the ground by his neck and slamming my fist into his terrified black face. "Worthless piece of scum. Your day just got real shitty." I punctuated my words with vicious blasts to his cheekbone and eye socket.

Shrieking, out of their minds, the other students in the class scattered toward the walls. Drafting tables flew into the bodies of bystanders, knocking some to the floor, as I held my target down and began choking him with the bottom rung of the stool he'd been sitting on seconds earlier.

In a flash, the wrestling coach and Johnny Holmes, the head security guard, who'd seen me barge in as they were meeting just steps away down the hall, pounced on me to try to pull me off. I fought back against them relentlessly while my adversary lay curled in a fetal heap beneath me. A row of art supply shelves and a dozen jars full of acrylic paint came crashing down around us, creating a furious Jackson Pollackesque array of rainbow mayhem.

"Get the hell off me," I grunted as the two large black men struggled to lift me to my feet. While I attempted to evade their grasp, I punctuated each profanity coming from my mouth with stomps to this kid's throat. Because I was younger and accustomed to grappling, they couldn't pull me away until I decided I'd caused enough damage.

When I'd had enough, they yanked me to my feet and half shoved, half dragged me out of the classroom and down the hall back to the principal's office. "I understand you made some dreadful remarks," my principal said. I could tell by her shaking black hands that she was trying hard to hold in her contempt for me. "Want to tell me why you would say such deplorable things, Mr. Picciolini?"

I erupted with a barrage of hate so venomous that if the spit that formed from my words had landed on an open wound on her body, she would have been poisoned on the spot. "I don't have to tell you shit," I seethed. "Fuck you, you filthy nigger bitch. You can take your bleeding-heart, liberal bullshit and stick it up your fat black cunt." I inched toward her with each toxic stab of my tongue. "I run this godforsaken school whether I'm in it or not. So, fuck you! Expel me!"

The black security guard who'd dragged me into her office leaped to wedge himself between us. He tore his glasses off his face and slammed them down on the principal's desk so hard that he mangled the frame and sent one of the shattered lens fragments flying toward the ceiling. Ready to take me on, he got so close to my face that I could smell the mustard from his lunch.

"Who you calling nigger, son?" he barked, grabbing me by the shirt and slamming me back against the wall, knocking me on my ass. "Know who the real nigger is? You!" Angry projectiles of saliva shot out with every other word. "I stood up against ignorant people like you and beat down your racist kind in the sixties on the streets of Chicago and, with God as my witness, I'll do the same now if I have to."

I was on my feet before he finished his sentence. But as I rose up he threw me back down and immobilized me by pressing his strong body against mine, his arms locked around my elbows, keeping me pinned between the wall and a tall metal file cabinet in the corner of the office. It was the first time someone had successfully physically humiliated me, besides my father.

The frightened principal picked up the phone and dialed 911. Within minutes, a police siren was wailing outside the building. "We'll see who gets arrested," I spit. "You can't abuse a student like this. Your black asses are all going to jail and getting fired. You'll be sorry!"

When the two Blue Island police officers rushed into the room, they threw me down to the ground and pressed their knees into the small of my back and neck while they wrenched my arms behind me and handcuffed my wrists. After they jerked me to my feet, the two of them marched me down the hallway toward the main entrance of the school where their flashing squad car was parked.

As if by design, the bell signaling the end of class rang, and students began pouring into the hallway at the same exact moment we exited the office. Their innocent chatter stopped as they saw the cops leading me out. The dense crowd parted to clear a path, and I suddenly felt like a young Robert De Niro in the grand finale scene of a Martin Scorsese gangster flick as the needle dropped into the opening grooves of a Rolling Stones tune. Everything moved in slow motion, and friendly hands reached out to pat my back, some outstretched in Nazi salute to encourage me. Others threw poisonous stares of contempt at the condemned man being led to the gallows.

The flash of inspiration hit me when I was listening to Skrewdriver: music was the secret, the missing piece for spreading our white-power gospel and expanding the movement. Why hadn't I thought about getting in on the skinhead music action myself? Now that so many of the pioneering white-power bands of the eighties were either defunct or based overseas, it was a wide-open market. I jotted down lyrics, making up choruses in my head, tried them out in front of the mirror.

"A band?" my mother asked when I announced I'd be practicing in the basement and we'd be making some noise. "But you aren't a musician. You quit piano lessons when you were ten."

"This is different. This is real music. Music people will listen to. Something that matters."

"I'll listen to your band, Buddy," my little brother chimed in.

"What instrument will you play?" my mom said. "You don't even have a harmonica. Or are you going to bang on pans like when you were a little boy?"

Buddy pulled two long wooden spoons from the utensil drawer and started to bang them on the counter like drumsticks.

"I'll find other people to play the instruments. I'll sing and write the lyrics. I'm the one who makes things happen."

Her ears perked up. She liked the sound of that. I traded my old punk rock record collection for some microphones, cables, and a beat-up PA system from a bingo hall, easily talked a few of the local guys I knew who played instruments into forming a band, and our group was born. I modeled us after Skrewdriver with more of an American hardcore vibe than traditional British skinhead Oi! music.

I was the frontman. The rest of the band was made up of former Eisenhower classmates. Rick, a long-haired heavy-metal kid who'd taken years of lessons, agreed to play guitar. Larry, Rick's best friend, brought over his drum set. Davey, a promising skateboarder in the neighborhood and the only person I knew with an electric bass guitar, rounded out the group.

None of the other three were remotely skinheads or Nazis, but they were white-power sympathizers who hung around and partied with us on the weekends. They had no objection to racist lyrics since they were friends with many of the same people I knew from Blue Island and shared some of the same views about minorities that I did. They were all psyched to be in a band, and I convinced them the fastest way to get noticed was through playing skinhead music. "There's only one or two other white-power bands in the U.S. right now. We'll make history. The old British skinhead bands are folk heroes. We'll be better than them."

I pointed out that not all Skrewdriver songs were about hate. "They're about justice, man. They don't only do 'fuck-you-nigger' songs. They sing about white pride and patriotism, fighting against communism, breaking the capitalist system. That kind of knowledge can change the world. And we can be part of that."

Without much debate, I named us White American Youth—WAY for short. It was a perfect name, considering I was going to use our music to show other white kids the *way* out of their sleepwalk.

We took up residence for the remainder of the winter in my basement pad, practicing, learning how to play together, imitating bands we liked by rehearsing their tunes, drinking, writing original songs. We'd stay up all hours, Buddy slipping in as often as he could to be part of this exciting new world.

"Hey, Buddy, can I sing into the microphone?" he'd ask me.

"I'm working right now. Maybe later." The look on his dejected face clearly displayed his hurt feelings. Sometimes I'd see him peeking through the window when we practiced. Once I caught him in the garage jumping around singing some of my lyrics into a flashlight.

My father would come down when we got really loud or if it was too late, telling us to shut up.

"Leave us the fuck alone," I'd say. "Go back upstairs." The rest of the guys in the band would watch with their mouths wide open as my father obeyed, cursing me under his breath. I was relentless in my perseverance to piss off my dad. For whatever reason, I resented him for not being there for me when I was a kid more than I did my mother, and it seemed I never stopped acting out against him.

My time for music was curtailed in February when Ombudsman Alternative School agreed to let me enroll and finish out my remaining credits to graduate. Still, school was never a priority for me, and I made time for WAY.

Ombudsman was a privately run remedial alternative education school with all of fifty kids in the whole student body. We were a mix of degenerates, dumb kids who couldn't read, gangbangers, drug dealers, and the hopeless cases everyone had given up on. Who'd given up on themselves.

The teachers figured out pretty fast that I could be an asset by helping them tutor students and reduce their workload. A smart kid like me with all those advanced high school classes under his belt, all I had to do was show up and help them administer basic spelling tests from time to time to graduate.

This was as close to acceptable as high school was ever likely to get. I wrote songs and even applied to a few colleges during classroom downtime. I figured I'd find hundreds more students to recruit on a university campus.

In the meantime, I focused on making music.

13

SICK SOCIETY

NOW THAT I WAS SEVENTEEN YEARS OLD and had my driver's license, I found lots of opportunities to go on road trips to meet skinheads from around the country whom I'd corresponded with. A new part-time job working at a pizza parlor in Beverly gave me the financial means, and some friends and I drove down to Georgia to hang out and network. One of the guys in my crew who'd recently been discharged from the army was dating a skinhead girl who lived there, and we stayed at a house in Marietta, Georgia, owned by a veteran Nazi skin named Teddy Dalrymple.

Marietta was one of the hottest places in the country for recruiting skinheads. It was almost child's play. White supremacy had been part of Marietta history ever since the Reconstruction-era Ku Klux Klan began immediately after the Civil War ended. It grew in popularity and remained ingrained as part of the local culture.

Dalrymple lived in a dilapidated wood-framed shanty at the end of Blanche Drive in Marietta that served as a bustling hub for Nazi youth activity throughout the Atlanta metropolitan area. At any given time you'd find dozens of kids hanging around for meetings, parties, rallies, and any number of other dubious activities. White-power skinheads passing through Georgia were always welcome to crash there, and

Christian Picciolini and the Marietta, Georgia, crew, 1990

Dalrymple made us feel right at home. He treated me as an equal and gave me tips on scaling our recruiting efforts outside of Chicago. He was a down-home Southern good ol' boy through and through, a funny guy with a round potbelly and giant muttonchops covering his cheeks. A redneck maverick, he had the line on every pro-white group in the country and was involved in organizing large-scale marches and protests in support of our cause.

It was at Dalrymple's house where I met Clay Wallaby, drummer for the legendary English skinhead band Condemned 84—one of my favorite Oi! bands, next to Skrewdriver. A great guy, he was an old-school British skin who had abandoned his home country and was building a new life with an American skinhead girl in Marietta. We hung out together some, drank lots of beer. I admired his musical ability and long-standing dedication to the skinhead scene. He was about more than getting into brawls and kicking ass.

"In order for the white race to prosper, mate," he warbled in his cockney accent, "for the next one hundred years we need to find ways to stick together and fight in a unified way to keep other races from pulling us apart or taking what is rightfully ours. Blacks and Third-World immigrants come to England and America in droves to leech from our resources, leaving little to nothing for us native blokes."

Clay was right. It was hard enough for the average American white family to keep their head above water without other races punching holes in our buckets and drawing from the same limited water well. After pausing to sip from his Carling lager, he went on to say, "Nationalism and ethnic purity are the single most important tenets of National Socialism."

It was what Clark had taught me early on about Nazi philosophies.

"Without those two things, a society becomes weak and diseased and impossible to cure," I agreed.

Over the last few years, I'd learned to believe that American multiculturalism meant we had no solid foundation to build a healthy civilization on top of. We were a sick society and whites were being killed off by "diversity." If we didn't start taking care of our own kind in this country, instead of the foreigners who stole our jobs and milked our infrastructure and resources, we were doomed. There simply wasn't enough to go around.

I enjoyed talking Nazi politics with Clay. He was genuinely passionate about National Socialism and music, and put them together well for more than a decade. As I do of so many others I met in my journey through the dark dens of white supremacy, I wonder whether Clay ever awakened to the error of his ways and got out. I hope for his own sake that he did.

By the time we'd left, I'd made connections through Clay and Teddy that would seriously help put WAY on the national radar. My goal—my dream—was to play a concert outside of Chicago with Minnesota white-power heavyweights Bound For Glory. Clay promised to make an introduction, as he had become friendly with the guys in the band. With this new contact, I was damn sure I'd find a way to get us together.

Teddy Dalrymple and I sat drinking cold beers on his front porch, the Georgia air dense with heat and humidity. "This here is an AR-15 semi-automatic assault weapon," he said, "that I nigger-rigged to fire full auto when you flip this dang switch." Dalrymple tossed me the weapon.

"Whoa... what the hell, Teddy?" I barely caught the flying rifle, spilling beer all over my Levis. "Is it loaded?" I was unsure of exactly how to hold it, nervous with its surprising weight.

"What good would it damn be if it ain't?" he said, winking at me. He stuffed tobacco into his carved corncob smoking pipe.

I felt the slick blue steel in my hands and studied it, running my fingers along the thick, ridged barrel. It was solid, heavy. Spent gunpowder residue from the weapon's body rubbed off onto my fingertips. The familiar burnt charcoal and earth smell sent me back to the Fourth of July fireworks displays I'd attended with the High Street Boys in my youth on the hill next to the football field behind Eisenhower. Images of those years, of the moments sitting with Buddy, came back, and I pushed them out of my mind.

Dalrymple reached over and snapped back the charging handle on the rifle and released it with a loud metallic clank. "There, it's chambered. Now point it at something that ain't white and squeeze the dang trigger." He chuckled.

"What?" I wasn't sure if I'd heard him correctly. I let out a nervous laugh.

"I said find something that ain't worth a shit and squeeze the fucking trigger! Is you motherfuckin' deaf, Yankee?" He grabbed me by the shoulder and forced me down into a kneeling position and pressed the stock against my cheek.

"Careful... it's loaded," I stammered.

"You see that nasty white whore over yonder with that half-breed baby?" He pointed to the middle of the block at a young white woman strapping her dark-skinned child into a stroller. "Shoot her in the face! Right between her nigger-lovin' eyes. Then shoot the li'l nigglet while you're at it."

My sweat glands hit overdrive, and I could feel my armpits instantly becoming cool and damp. My blood ran cold. Sweat streaked down my forehead and stung my eyes. "You're joking, right? That is pretty funny, Teddy." I laughed it off and attempted to set down the rifle.

"Does it look like I'm yanking your chain, boy?" He pulled out a shiny pistol from his waistband and pressed it firmly against my temple. "Now aim."

Frozen in place, my stomach churning, I was ready to expel the loads of smothered, chunked, and chili-topped Waffle House hash browns I'd scarfed down for lunch.

The cold steel he had placed against the side of my face assured me he was dead serious. I felt I had no choice. "Okay, okay, Teddy. Just relax." I slowly turned my head, lowered my cheek to meet the weapon's stock, zeroing the sights in on the unsuspecting woman's forehead as best as I could. I saw her smiling and teasing the young infant. Laughing.

"Now pull the dang trigger, cowboy."

I tried hard to keep my hands from trembling.

"Squeeze the fucking trigger or I will! Is you a cop, motherfucker?"

I took in a shallow breath, intentionally jerking my arm to the right to assure I'd miss her, and pulled the trigger.

Click!

Dalrymple let out a loud, guttural smoker's laugh and hacked uncontrollably for a moment while slapping me on the back. "I got you, man!" He took the pistol that had been resting against my temple and brought it to his face. When he pulled back the trigger, it spit out a short blue flame that he used to light his pipe.

"What the fuck, Teddy?"

More unholy laughter and coughing. "Had to make sure you wasn't some kinda lawman or undercover fed. You think I'd give you a loaded gun? Shit, you ought to see your dang baby face, Al Capone."

"You're an asshole." I cracked a tense smile as I dropped the butt of the heavy weapon into his wide-open lap, hitting him hard in the nuts in the process.

He yelped and doubled over. "Owwweee! Why the hell'd you go do that for?"

"Just had to make sure you weren't some kind of queer," I quipped. My arms felt like Jell-O as I wrenched open the screen door to head back inside the shack. "I needed to know I didn't have some sort of a faggot fighting next to me when the time comes." I wiped my brow.

I came away from the trip feeling both anxious about my involvement in the movement outside of Chicago and certain that the time had come for me to start loading up on weapons myself. I was convinced there was a race war brewing, and soon. If we didn't protect ourselves, we'd be overrun. I was a white warrior willing to stand as a vanguard against that threat. I'd be ready. And heavily armed.

Sometime during the subsequent months, a fellow Hammerskin from Montreal visited Chicago and wanted to set up a meeting to introduce me to Wolfgang Droege, a radical Canadian KKK leader who'd been heating things up across the border, and Don Black, a militant Klansman from Alabama. He tried to draw me in by saying that Libya's Muslim dictator Muammar Gaddafi had sent a government attaché to meet with Droege and Black about giving North American neo-Nazis some financial backing. "Wolfie wants the Chicago Hammerskins in on it," he said.

I suppose I didn't particularly care if Gaddafi wasn't white. He despised the Jews as much as we did. And if this could help bankroll a weapons arsenal, that'd be a good thing. Gaddafi wanted to meet serious anti-Israel American militants. He wanted to fly us over to Libya to discuss a strategy and support our cause by seeding us with cash.

This was big time. As serious as it could get.

I said I'd think about it, uncertainty hitting me like a cinder block. The Canadian Hammerskin hounded me, pressured me, insisting this was our big chance. I knew Droege and Black, allegedly with the help of Klan leader David Duke, had previously organized a failed military coup on the Caribbean island of Dominica, and the two had gone to prison for it. That kind of adventure was intense and appealed to me, but I was terrified of getting caught.

What if it was a setup? I wondered. I didn't know these guys or the Canadian skinhead very well. If I agreed to the plan and the feds caught wind of it, I'd certainly be convicted as a traitor to the United States, a crime punishable by death, not prison time. I loved my country, I just didn't agree with those currently in power—the system that held us down. I was willing to take on the government on my terms. Was this the way to do it?

"He wants to give us a million dollars," pleaded the Montreal Hammerskin. "Think of all the weapons we can buy with that kind of money. The damage we can do."

He was coming on too strong. "So why don't you go?" I asked.

"Wolfgang specifically asked for Clark Martell. When I told him he was in prison, he asked for the next in command."

"Tell Wolfgang I appreciate the offer, but I'll have to pass this time," I said. "I don't have a passport." I lied.

So I respectfully declined and kept my involvement domestic for the time being.

A year later Droege and his cohorts ended up in federal prison because the whole Gaddafi deal had been a sting operation set up by the Canadian Security Intelligence Service—CSIS.

There were plenty of conflicts to focus on closer to home. Like the pack of black gangbangers who had been accosting Pecker and Chili, two of the Beverly guys, every day on the city bus they rode home from school. This infuriated the hell out of all of us, so we planned our ambush. Pecker and Chili would stand up to them on the bus, talk trash, and get them all riled up. They'd lure them off at their stop to fight. And we'd be there waiting.

Worked like a charm. Half a dozen of us hid around the corner behind the diner near the bus stop. When the three gangbangers got off the bus, we waylaid their black asses and beat the shit out of them in the middle of rush hour on busy Western Avenue. Cars screeched to a halt all around us, as we dragged the three guys out to the middle of the street, beating them without mercy. Car horns blared and people screamed, but I didn't give a shit.

Kubiak grabbed a handful of Afro on one of the guys and was swinging him around, off the ground, like an Olympic hammer thrower.

Three Beverly Boys had another pinned down and pummeled him with a barrage of kicks to his stomach and back. His wails were louder than the car horns that were begging them to stop.

I chased the remaining thug on foot and caught him in the alley behind the diner. I football-tackled him into a row of garbage cans and drove my elbow into his nose, breaking it with a resonating crack, as my feet suddenly shot out from under me. I'd slipped in a slick puddle of discarded restaurant grease, lost my grip, and the guy got away. The rest of the guys didn't back off until they heard the flurry of police sirens approaching. Then we all climbed over cars—denting their shiny hoods with our boots—to get the hell out of there. Last thing I needed with assault charges already looming over me was to be busted for a race-inspired fight, a felony hate crime.

We made it back to my house without incident, laughing all the way, mimicking the muds begging for us to stop. Suffice it to say, those kids never rode that bus again.

Not long after the Western Avenue bus incident, I appeared in court for sentencing on trumped-up charges against me for allegedly assaulting an anti-racist punk named Hector Diaz. The irony was that the one time I was charged with assaulting someone in the years of doing it, I was certain I'd never come to blows with this accuser before. I dressed appropriately. Used my finest manners. "Yes-judged" that black-robed clown to death. I was sentenced to six months of court supervision.

Because I was under supervision, I had to refrain from getting arrested during that time. So, I shifted my focus and injected more venom into my music, got downright aggressive about rehearsals, and in May of 1991, we proudly gave our first live concert in a place called the Barn, a community center in Blue Island. At a birthday party, of all things. I didn't particularly care for the venue, but it was exciting having people responding to our music, getting revved up, cheering for us.

The tiny place was jam-packed with a couple dozen kids, and the crowd was loving us. The scent of pine from the wood-clad walls was overshadowed by the pungent odors of floor wax and teen sweat. The unsuspecting parents were getting drunk in the parking lot while we entertained the sixteen-year-old birthday girl and a roomful of new recruits with our rendition of several Skrewdriver anthems and a few WAY originals.

We're the warriors of the street
With shaven heads and boots on our feet
We stand tall like a stone wall
Against all evil we won't fall
WAY's our name, white power we follow
We're the White American Youth of tomorrow!

The room whirled with teen angst and perspiration. Choppy guitar rhythms and the rousing choruses drove the moist juvenile bodies violently into one another from every direction.

With only a month left until graduation, I drove to Ombudsman in the clunky 1984 Chevy truck my parents helped me buy so I could travel the extra distance to alternative school. As I pulled into the parking lot, I saw my old skinhead pal Craig Sargent, who by now had also been kicked out of Marist and Eisenhower for his racist activities, locked in a shoving match with two black students. I jammed on my brakes, skidded to a stop, and jumped into the fray.

Craig and I beat up this fat dude named Pooky and his wiry sidekick, Juice, before they even had a chance to so much as utter our names. I pulled the bigger of the two off Craig, while he continued to pound the other. As a crowd, including the teachers, gathered in the parking lot, we continued to volley blows after they attempted to retreat into the building. We threw them against parked cars and knocked them to the ground repeatedly.

Having no doubt our efforts would mean we were both kicked out of yet another school and the cops would be looking for us, we hopped into my truck and took off, spending the rest of the day parked in a forest preserve drinking the warm beer I had stashed under my seat.

Four weeks to graduation.

Sure enough, I was reported and expelled. Five schools in four years.

My parents begged the school board president for a favor one final time and were granted a special reprieve to enroll me in the local community college to finish my remaining two high school credits.

"You're ruining your life," my dad said. "I know you think you know it all and believe you have everything under control, but..."

"Stop pretending like you fucking care. You don't! You never have." I managed to get the words out while holding back tears of anger at his very suggestion that he knew a damn thing about me or what I was feeling. "I do what I want, when I want. And you haven't earned the right to tell me what to do."

Just then seven-year-old Buddy walked into the room, holding a mangled wrestling action figure. He'd pulled the head off it and the plastic body was riddled with cut marks, rendering it almost unrecognizable as the former figure of black WWF professional wrestler Junkyard Dog.

"Look, Buddy," he beamed. "It's a dead nigger."

My mother ripped it from his pudgy fingers as both she and my brother wailed.

My dad's angry eyes penetrated mine. "See what you've done?"

Knowing my time in school was coming to an end, I considered joining the military. I'd receive excellent combat training there. My fighting skills would only improve, and I'd get to handle the best weapons known to mankind. I knew I could rise to a leadership position quickly and influence trained warriors to join our movement. And frankly, the promise of self-righteous violence appealed to me.

I headed over to the army office to enlist. "I want to be an MP," I told the recruiter.

He took one look at my skinhead clothes and tattoos and shook his head. "You can't be military police. People like you have one choice: infantry."

"People like me?"

"I know your kind. Tough, brazen, and you have a taste for blood. Front line for you all the way."

This grunt wasn't going to send me packing. "Fine. Infantry it is. I'll work my way up the ranks."

"Of course you will, private," he said, and signed me up for the ASVAB test, the aptitude and enlistment exam for the U.S. military.

When my scores came back, the recruiter changed his tune. He said I'd scored higher than any of his previous enlistees ever had. "Son," he said, "you still want to be an MP? Let's get you that job."

Only problem was, I wasn't old enough. At seventeen I still needed a parent's signature.

When I told her I wanted to join the army, my mother was beside herself. She didn't want me killed. "You have a long life ahead of you. Why go fight in wars that have nothing to do with us?" My father agreed. Buddy liked the idea of having a brother who was a soldier and brought out his GI Joe dolls and asked me to show him how I'd kill the bad guys. My mother snatched the dolls away and told him to go watch something nice on television.

My mom brought my grandparents in as a last resort to try to dissuade me. She knew I still had a soft spot for Nonna and Nonno and wouldn't lose my temper if they were there.

My grandmother tried to convince me to change my mind. "Christian, why don't you go to school or find a nice job instead? You're such a good boy," she pleaded. "War is not a good place for anyone. Ask Nonno. He can tell you." Her motherly warmth and calmness were always so comforting. I suddenly missed them.

As Nonna played my surrogate mother growing up, the adopted fatherly responsibilities fell to my grandfather, Nonno. But not even his dreadful firsthand accounts of his time fighting in the Second World War could dissuade me once I'd made up my mind to enlist.

A man of few words, Nonno interrupted my grandmother. "It's not a place for you. You have a good heart." I wasn't so sure. "You will come back different."

I was counting on that.

Respecting my grandparents and their wishes was something I had done without question when I was a small child, and I also understood that they were wiser than either of my parents—or me, for that matter. But the world was a different place than the one they'd known in the old country at my age. I envied my grandfather for going to war, serving as a bombardier under Mussolini in far-off places like Egypt and Libya and Belgium. I respected that, and I wanted to earn the same type of respect he had.

We were already in a constant war within our own borders, regardless of whether we wore military camouflage and desert boots or a bomber jacket and Doc Martens. I would go to the army and come back stronger. Tougher. Smarter. And more equipped to fight my own battles. I railed hard against my family's wishes, driven by the belief that I knew something they didn't.

Eventually, they all caved.

And so the day came. I waited for the recruiter to pick me up and take me in for my army physical and have my parents sign off on my enlistment form. But he was late.

Half an hour late.

An hour.

I called the recruiting office to see what the holdup was. It seemed my recruiter had been reassigned to another post in Albuquerque two days earlier. "But don't worry, young man, we'll send someone else to come over to pick you up right away," the staff sergeant assured me.

"Don't bother," I said indignantly. "Fuck you people."

It felt good saying that to the government.

Meanwhile, at the community college where I'd started my final course to earn my high school diploma, to my amazement, school was actually interesting. I was taking Criminal Justice 101 to fulfill my remaining two credits. It struck me as cool to have a class ending in 101. For the first time, I was treated as an adult inside an institution of learning. It was college. An open campus. Nobody was shoving rules down my throat. Teachers never insisted I show up or forced me go to detention for not doing homework or for cutting a class that bored me to death.

Without much effort, I aced the course. I, a mere high school senior, a truant and delinquent and menace, was, I learned, the only one in my entire college class to get an A. It felt good. Real good. It was the first time in my whole student life a grade meant something to me. I had to bite my lip when the professor talked about the demographics of race in the prison system and the lopsided incarceration ratio of blacks to whites, but it was tolerable. I could have explained the reasons for this better than he did. But I didn't.

At the end of the semester, I'd completed the credit requirements, and I was eligible to receive my high school diploma.

But I could not participate in the graduation ceremony, which was taking place at Eisenhower.

The school had filed for an order of protection—a restraining order—against me. The directive was to arrest me on sight if I stepped foot on school property.

And so my high school years came unceremoniously to an end.

SKINHEADS AGAINST
SHARP

14

HEAVY-METAL HATE MACHINE

I HAD TO EXPAND MY BASE—IT wasn't enough to pick up kids around Blue Island anymore—which meant it was time to focus more on my band. No doubt music could make me stronger than ever. With school a thing of the past, we could start performing at rallies outside of Chicago, inciting people on a larger scale. Maybe even Europe.

So I threw myself into WAY, lining up whatever gigs I could. I spent hours writing new lyrics, figuring out beats, piecing together songs from the few guitar chords I knew. Music was a means to an end, the end being more control. Respect.

Our second show was in the living room of a local skinhead's home, filled with teenagers, cheap wood paneling, and linoleum floors. There was a mix of Blue Island skins and Beverly guys, and Kubiak was there entertaining some of the younger female recruits. Goth girls. WAY had only been together for six months, but it didn't matter. We just had to play fast and loud and get people moving and we'd be fine. There'd be beer too, which always helps make marginal musicians sound good.

It took only a verse of provoking words and a few power chords into the first tune to win the crowd's approval. They were slam-dancing, thrusting out their arms in Nazi salutes, nodding their heads aggressively

Christian Picciolini, White American Youth rehearsal and confiscated SHARP patch, 1991.

to the beat, motivated by our songs. My words. It was an intensely powerful feeling. We were a movement united through music, and I'd never felt anything like it.

I could have sung all night.

But around midnight a beer bottle came crashing through the front window of the house. We dropped our instruments and filed out into the front yard looking for revenge. Across the street appeared a cadre of dark silhouettes, wearing black hoodies pulled over their heads and hockey and ski masks to cover their faces. Bats, chains with padlocks, lead pipes, and hockey sticks were clutched in their hands. It was an ambush.

Antis, young and old, male and female, surrounded us from about thirty yards away, backlit by a glowing amber porch light. The rest of our troops from inside joined us on the lawn. The tension hovered, approaching DEFCON Level One, itchy fingers at the ready on the nuclear button. At least twenty of us lined up, ready to do battle, the fury of the music still drumming in our heads.

Another bottle crashed at Kubiak's feet, spraying shards of glass against his fourteen-eyelet oxblood boots. We breathed one heaving collective breath and, as if a battle horn had sounded, charged the opposition, sprinting at full speed into the night. One line of warriors set to clash with the enemy.

Most of the opposition retreated, scattering at the sight of fury on our faces. We flew full-speed and caught up before they made it to the corner. Some had shown up solely to intimidate us through a show of numbers. They had no courage to fight. They fled like cowards.

Others turned and stood their ground. They put up a strong fight. Knuckles connected with noses, jaws, and cheekbones. Cries of pain and attrition filled the air as we struck each other down, like avenging angels in Doc Marten boots.

I turned from one person to another, punching with all my power. This was the enemy. No mercy.

I swung around and came face-to-face with April Crenshaw. She and her husband, Jerry, were the leaders of SHARP in Chicago, but he'd run off and left her there to fend for herself.

She read the rage in my eyes. Tears and mascara mixed and began rolling murky black streaks down her face as she backpedaled, pleading for me not to hurt her.

I'd never hit a girl, but she needed to learn a lesson. So instead I tore her SHARP patch from her bomber jacket. My trophy. Better than drawing blood. And to humiliate her further, I made her hand over her Docs. No skinhead ever gives up their boots. I took a box cutter to the laces. She slid them off and handed them over to me in a final recognition of her defeat. A crowd of my soldiers gathered.

She rose, barefoot in fishnet stockings. I resisted an urge to kick her symbolically in her ass as she retreated. Off she went, a skinhead specter disappearing into the solitary night.

We'd beaten down her anti-racist crew, our main adversaries in Chicago. And without so much as laying a finger on her, I'd disgraced their leader, more of a blow than any physical injury we'd caused.

Police sirens ripped through the darkness, and when the first wave of cops arrived they arrested what remaining SHARP skins were lying around, for criminal damage to property. The ones who didn't run were covered in bruises, some unable to get to their feet.

Kubiak's friendly hand reached out to pull me out of the fray. "Get inside. Away from the cops. Danny's on his way and said he'd take care of it."

I retreated inside the house. When the police banged on the door looking for me, I was nowhere to be seen.

"We didn't do anything, officer," I hear one of our girls say. "Just having a small get-together, and then a bottle flew through the window..."

"Where's Picciolini, smartass?" the lead detective asked, pushing his body past the girl in the doorway to give Kubiak a friendly pat on the shoulder.

"Ain't seen him, Danny," Kubiak replied.

"Haven't seen him, huh? You better get home before Mom and Dad find out what you've been up to tonight," he whispered. It was his brother, who worked as a police detective in Blue Island. "And tell your idiot pal hiding in the closet to stay off the streets for a while."

"Yes, sir, Officer Kubiak," the younger Kubiak quipped.

"Have a good night, *Mein Führer*," I said from behind the closet door.

A few days later I decided to make a mark of a different sort. Every kid in the area knew me and in a sense respected me, but I now wanted the respect due me from adults, the very people whose children I was trying to protect.

I entered a car in the spectator's derby held at Raceway Park, the same racetrack where I'd flyered cars in the early days before Clark was sent to prison. The attendance would make for good exposure.

I bought an olive green, four-door Chevy Caprice Classic junker from Kubiak's redneck neighbor and set to work making my car the most striking heavy-metal hate machine anybody would ever see. I'd gotten a small raise at the pizza job and picked up a few extra nights a week. The car cost me a hundred and fifty bucks—half of a week's pay—but the attention it would get would be worth so much more.

I painted it matte black with a roller and house paint, except for "88," Hitler's number, in white on the doors. Nazi SS lightning bolts were in red on the rear quarter panels, two crossed hammers rising from flames spray painted on the hood. "White Pride" in large letters emblazoned across the back bumper. It was a badass car with a powerful message. Like Carmine's. I had no doubt I'd win the derby, and my cause would be further spotlighted in the news. White power would rule.

One of the few requirements for getting on the track, aside from removing all windows but the windshield, was that cars had to have a metal bar welded along the inside of the driver's door for safety. This presented a problem because, oddly enough, there wasn't a welder among my wide range of blue-collar acquaintances. I can't tell you how many people I asked, how many leads I followed, how many phone calls I made and doors I knocked on in vain. I was determined to get my car into that derby and broadcast our message and, by doing so, demonstrate that white people shouldn't be scared to stand up for themselves.

While I worked on the heap and continued my search for a welder, the painted car sat in plain view in the driveway. My parents weren't remotely happy about it, but, as usual, they backed down.

The marked-up race car attracted a ton of attention, though, exactly as I wanted it to, and soon enough a CBS news crew came out to the house to do a story on it.

Nonno, my elderly grandfather, who lived across the street, was outside tending to his yard when the news van showed up, and a cameraman and reporter piled out.

He dropped his gardening tools and approached the commotion as they surrounded my car in the driveway. He barely spoke English. They descended on him and shoved a camera and microphone in his face.

"Do you know who this car belongs to? How do you feel about having this type of racism in your neighborhood? Is this crossing the First Amendment freedom of speech line?"

My grandfather might not have understood English well, but he certainly understood the frenetic attitude, and he knew they weren't there to give me any awards for my artistic creation. It had been four years since I'd paid much attention to him or Nonna. I thought I was too busy to look after them, despite there only being a hundred feet between us.

But I was his grandson, and nothing else mattered. "Go," he said in his broken English. "He is good boy. Go away. Leave alone! Go! Now!"

And so this frail old man from Italy drove the buzzards away.

They didn't come back.

He never said a word about it to me, and my car continued to stand proudly in my parents' driveway, steadily gathering public nuisance citations from the city. I eventually gave up on finding a welder and sold the car for sixty bucks to another kid on the block, who painted over everything I'd done and raced it in the derby.

I didn't bother to find out how he'd finished, but I was sure he hadn't done well. He'd robbed the car of all its power.

ITE AMERICA

15

AKA PABLO

I PURCHASED MY NEXT GUN UNLAWFULLY and without a permit. Ironically, I bought it off the street from a Mexican. It was a .380-caliber semiautomatic handgun. I threw the old, busted .25 that Kubiak had given me into the Blue Island canal one night after failing to get it to chamber ammunition properly.

Until you grip a loaded gun in your hand, you don't know power. It's a surreal feeling.

Holding my pistol, I felt I could conquer the world.

I loved it.

I talked to Bill Rudolph—an older Chicago Nazi whom I'd originally met through Clark and Carmine—about getting more guns. He worked on a factory assembly line, like a true-blue American would, and responded by giving me a co-worker's stolen wallet, complete with Illinois driver's license.

"Use this," he told me. "First thing you gotta do is get a permit to buy a gun."

I didn't look a thing like the chubby Latino guy on the stolen license and pointed it out.

He scoffed at my inexperience. "You think anybody gives a shit if that's you or not? You fill out a firearm application and go to the ghetto to have

Christian Picciolini, local newspaper clipping, 1991

some stoned, fat baby mama notarize it. She won't even look at the picture on the license. They collect the money and don't ask any questions."

I couldn't believe that would be the case, but I'd be damned if I'd show any fear. What's the worst they could do? Call the cops and charge me for having a stolen ID? It's not as if the cops and I were strangers. Like Bill promised, the black lady behind the currency exchange counter was so preoccupied talking on the phone to her friend that she didn't so much as glance at the ID. She did, however, take my money and stamp her approval on my firearm application.

I brought the paperwork back, and I showed Bill. "So now what?"

"Send the notarized application in to the Illinois State Police and..."

"State police?" I interrupted, "What do you mean state police? I thought that was it. She stamped it... See?"

"Don't worry about it. It's not your name or photo. The address won't even be yours."

"But isn't that a federal crime? Like mail fraud or something?" I could tell he was starting to lose patience with me.

"Look, just give me the damn paperwork, and I'll send it in for you." He took me to his living room window and pulled aside the curtain. "You see that vacant house across the street? We'll use that address. When the mail gets delivered, I'll grab it for you. Don't worry."

"All right." It sounded like a valid theory. "Then what?"

"Go to a gun show, Pablo Ortiz." We both laughed.

I swear I looked nothing like the guy in the stolen driver's license. And for two solid months I worried the FBI and ATF would knock down my door and arrest me for federal fraud and firearm violations.

Gun shows were everywhere. I found one soon after Bill received the approved "Pablo Ortiz" firearm permit in the mail from the Illinois State

Police, and we headed to the show without a qualm. I had my gun license and Bill's reassurance that the racist hillbillies at these shows didn't give a damn whom they sold the guns to. It was about the green. So long as you looked white.

Bill was right again. The people at this show—and every other gun show I attended—couldn't care less whom they sold weapons to. The guy he introduced me to, an older family friend of his, barely looked at the permit, aside from scribbling its info on the receipt. Even the mandatory federal waiting period didn't seem to bother this guy. The seller handed over the gun the second he collected my money.

I left that first show with a brand new Ruger 9mm pistol tucked into the waistband of my jeans, electrified by the sheer power of it. I was ready for anything now.

The only thing I lacked was training.

So I went to the shooting range, where no questions were asked. Give them the money, flash your permit, your white smile and go.

I picked up shooting quickly. My finger squeezed the trigger with ease, my arm supported the weapon without flinching, my eye zeroed in on the target within a fraction of a second.

Like most sports I tried, shooting was relatively easy for me. But shooting would not be a sport.

It was a part of my survival plan. I was prepared to battle to the death, even martyr myself, to protect the white race from destruction.

I saved money from every paycheck and acquired more firearms from these gun shows. At seventeen years old, my arsenal consisted of a new Russian-made AK-47, a Ruger 9mm, a .380 semi-auto handgun, a military-issue .30-caliber M-1 carbine rifle with a folding carbon stock, and, for good measure, a sawed-off 20-gauge shotgun that was cut down to about the length of my forearm.

By fall, I was a decent shot and had collected weapons and ammo to spare. I was ready. I didn't brag about my cache, but word somehow got around. Cops suspected I had illegal weapons but couldn't prove it based on only hearsay. They had no concrete evidence to ask a judge for a warrant to search my house.

I usually kept a loaded handgun on me when I was away from home, but this had a strange effect. In addition to making me feel powerful, it made me very paranoid. Anything could happen. Circumstances could turn ugly fast, and I knew it wouldn't take much provocation for me to stick it in someone's face. I had a recurring nightmare in which I was forced to pull it out and had to use it—I wouldn't dare not use it and appear weak. That scared the shit out of me.

One evening I got home from work long after midnight, stripped down to my boxers, and got into bed. But as I began drifting off, a noise outside my window jolted me awake.

Kubiak and I had started a lot of fights in the previous week. Had one of our victims come by to get revenge?

I rolled out of my bed and crawled across the floor to my dresser. I reached behind it and moved my hand along the wall until I felt the wood stock of my sawed-off shotgun.

From a distance, I saw the intruder's backlit silhouette against the window. Someone was trying to break in. Creeping along the wall, I contemplated every possible scenario. What if they had a gun? What if it was the cops? I took in a deep breath and filled my lungs. Exhaled. I flung the curtain open, weapon ready to explode.

The terrified face meeting the barrel of my shotgun wasn't that of an enemy.

It was my mother's.

Horror and frustration flooded me. What was she doing spying on me in the middle of the night? Why couldn't she leave me the fuck alone? My finger had been heavy on that trigger. "Christian," she cried. "It's me, Mamma. My God!"

I lowered the shotgun. Trembling, I lifted open the window.

"Jesus fucking Christ! You can't sneak up on me like that! What the hell are you doing?"

She sank down into the bushes weeping and quivering. "Why do you have a gun? What life are you living?"

My mother dropped to her knees and wailed, covering her face with her shaking hands. She prayed to God.

"Don't worry about it. It's for protection. That's all. Just in case." I was genuinely sorry.

"In case of what?" she cried, her eyes pleading. "What did you do to need this kind of protection?"

Any anger I felt toward her evaporated. Her fear and concern were so sincere, so heartfelt; I felt a stab of regret for all that I'd put her through. I felt my mother's sadness, I wanted to reach out and comfort her, hold her, and tell her it would be okay, that I loved and appreciated her. I knew she cared about me. I knew my father did too. But we'd grown so far apart.

"Mom, go to bed," I said. "It's late. No more crying now. Everything's okay." I shut the window and heard her continue to sob, followed by a fit of retching.

I stayed awake for hours trembling—shaken to my core and remorseful about how I'd come so close to killing my own mother. I had been just a nervous twitch away from blowing her head clean off her body. But every time I started to drift off, exhausted from my mind racing, the idea that I needed more guns woke me right back up. Tonight had proven that somebody could come for me anytime. I had to be better prepared.

A.Y.

16

MARTYR

In the midst of all the rallies and concerts, violence and guns, something very unexpected happened. I fell in love. Crazy wild in love.

Her name was Lisa, and she wanted nothing to do with me and what I stood for.

We met through mutual Beverly friends. I wasn't looking for anybody. My life was full of responsibilities to my crew, my time already claimed by writing and performing white-power music, and my head full of concerns about the endangered white race and the risks it faced.

I had a survival bag packed. Guns and ammunition. An escape plan. When ZOG's secret, shadow government launched their attack to enslave us, I would be ready to battle it head-on, to lead a blood-soaked revolution and become a martyr like Earl Turner had in *The Turner Diaries*.

A love affair wasn't necessarily part of the picture.

Sure, I had more than my fair share of "girlfriends" and casual sex, but I wasn't interested in anything serious.

When I first saw Lisa, I didn't pay much attention to her. She hung out on the periphery of the Beverly group, a nice little Irish, Catholic school girl who showed up at parties now and again with some of her high school girlfriends. She'd been a year behind me in school, so our social paths hadn't crossed often, but this time she caught my eye. So I asked her out.

"I was wondering if... maybe... I could take you to a movie or dinner or something. I hear that *Terminator 2* is supposed to be pretty fucking brutal..."

She said no.

No was a word I was unaccustomed to hearing. The people around me always said yes, and they said it quickly and followed it up with whatever action needed to happen.

I lost sleep over her response, trying to figure out how I'd put her off. Was it because she was still in high school for another year and I'd already graduated? Perhaps it was distance—we lived a few neighborhoods apart and she didn't have a car. Maybe she didn't like skinheads or my reputation as a fighter. Was it the movie? Maybe I should have suggested *Sleeping with the Enemy* instead.

I resolved to ask her out again.

Every time I asked her out, her answer was the same: a resounding no.

I was pissed.

"Send her some flowers, you jerk," one of my close female skinhead friends advised. "Show her you're more than a hardass. And stop suggesting guy movies. Ask her to see something nice and funny like *City Slickers* or some romantic comedy. She's probably a sweet innocent girl. You're running around kicking people's teeth in and getting in trouble with the law all the time. You gotta show her you're a good guy."

"Want to write me a letter of recommendation?" I joked.

"Seriously. Try sending flowers," she said.

So I sent a bouquet of red roses to Lisa's house. I'd like to say I sat back and waited, but that would be a lie. I obsessed over what to do next. Wait for her to make the next move? Call her and ask if she'd gotten them? Show up at her place like I had a right to be there?

I got my chance two weeks later when Lisa invited the Beverly gang over to her house for beers one night when her mom was out of town for work at a sales seminar. I saw this as my opportunity to cozy up to Lisa and convince her I had a soft side. I asked her what she thought of the roses I'd sent. She said they were nice, a sweet gesture. After a night of hanging out and talking about things that interested us both, like music and drawing, she decided to give me a chance and agreed to go out on a date the following week.

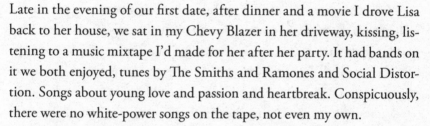

Late in the evening of our first date, after dinner and a movie I drove Lisa back to her house, we sat in my Chevy Blazer in her driveway, kissing, listening to a music mixtape I'd made for her after her party. It had bands on it we both enjoyed, tunes by The Smiths and Ramones and Social Distortion. Songs about young love and passion and heartbreak. Conspicuously, there were no white-power songs on the tape, not even my own.

A steady rainfall had begun, and the rhythm of the droplets pitter-pattering against the roof created a soothing cadence for our makeout session. Lisa's skin felt like silk on my fingertips and I worked hard to summon up my soft side, touching her face when we kissed, cradling her gently in my arms.

The humidity of the muggy August night and our steamy lip-lock caused the car windows to fog up, revealing several crude swastikas that Kubiak had traced with his finger on the inside of the windshield the week prior, while we'd been staking out a house in Blue Island that a group of SHARPs had rented to keep a closer eye on us. I leaned in and pulled Lisa close to shield her eyes, so that the markings wouldn't upset her. Not fast enough.

"Can I ask you something?" Lisa spoke timidly, pulling herself out of my arms. "Promise me you won't get mad."

"Of course." I reached to caress her hand. "What's wrong?"

Lisa sighed and moved her gaze away from mine. I could tell from her hesitation that she was about to ask me something that had been weighing heavily on her mind. "Why do you have so much hatred inside of you?"

I couldn't help but adjust myself in my seat to fend off her unsettling glare. At that moment, I would rather have been hit in the jaw with brass knuckles than been faced with that question. Especially from Lisa. It caught me off guard, but I knew I had to give her an answer if we were going to have any chance for a second date.

So I lied to her. "I don't hate anyone. I just love what I stand for so much that I'm willing to protect it from those who want to do it harm."

I knew my answer was bullshit. Instead of being honest with Lisa, I'd replied with the standard one-size-fits-all party rhetoric. It was a common practice within the movement to always spin our hateful agenda and wrap it in a pretty little "white pride" bow for the general public to consume. The truth was, we hated everybody who wasn't like us.

Without flinching, Lisa replied, "But then why aren't you doing anything positive? All you do is say such hateful things and get in horrible fights and hurt people. That's not love. That's violence and destruction and hate." Her eyes pleaded with mine for the truth. "When you're with me, you are so caring and gentle, but all I can wonder is, which one is the real you?"

The question made my throat catch. Even though I'd answered it without much hesitation dozens of times before—it would be posed by teachers and coaches—my response would usually be punctuated by the words *fuck you*. When the question left her soft lips, I suddenly couldn't muster the words to string together an answer that made much sense to me.

The cassette in the car stereo clicked and flipped to begin playing the first song from the B-side of the tape.

Lisa continued over the familiar twang of Social Distortion's guitars, "When you love something, how can you possibly do so at anyone else's expense?"

Her voice was tender. Caring. The dampness in the air turned the fogginess on the windows into streaking rivulets of water that raced toward the swastikas now swirling at the center of my mind. Her emerald eyes looked deep into mine as my stomach wrenched tighter. I looked to her and said, "I do it because it's important to me."

"Am I important to you?" she pleaded.

"Yes." The wind picked up and shook the truck violently, startling Lisa.

In the foreground, the porch light lit up, and we heard her mother call out. "They've issued a severe weather warning. You should come inside, Lisa."

"I guess I better go before the storm gets any worse. You should probably go too." She leaned in and kissed me on the lips. "Thanks for my mix tape."

With that, she threw open the door and darted for shelter. I watched as she gracefully dodged the raindrops and disappeared into the house. The swirling wind battering my truck was no match for the tempest brewing inside of me.

I spent every waking moment with Lisa and never wanted to leave her side. She was smart and creative. Aside from our political views clashing, we were otherwise perfectly matched. She was headstrong, but she trusted me and felt safe with me around.

Lisa eventually brought me home to meet her family, and they also began to like me. Her mother had been a hippie in the early seventies, but somehow me being a racist skinhead didn't appear to bother her much. Besides, she never seemed to tell Lisa no to anything. She treated her more like a companion than her daughter. Being accepted into Lisa's home made me feel like I was stable and part of something normal. Her mother had remarried, but her new husband was a bit of a slacker, so Lisa and her mom thought it was nice to have me in the house to repair things and help with the yard work. And it wasn't long before her little brother dressed the skinhead part.

Lisa was the first person I totally opened up to. I'd even held back from the High Street Boys, and I sure didn't confide my innermost feelings to any of my skinhead street soldiers. Leaders don't do that.

But Lisa and I had so much in common; we understood one other on a deeper level almost immediately. So we opened up and allowed ourselves to be vulnerable with each other.

Like me, she had been more or less raised by her grandparents, and her parents had played no significant role when she was a child. They were flower children who'd split up when it wasn't fun being together anymore. Lisa was only three at the time and her brother less than a year old. Her dad never looked back, so Lisa had no recollection of him.

Once she was on her own, Lisa's young mother had no choice but to adapt to the responsibility of being a single parent. She found her way into a corporate job that meant long hours and little time with her children.

Like me, Lisa spent most of her time with her grandparents while her mother, like mine, dedicated all her time to building a career.

Long before either of us ever thought of having children, Lisa and I would both promise each other that we'd never be like that with our own kids.

"Do you know how embarrassing it is that my girlfriends don't even know what my mother looks like?" Lisa would say. "I think half of them thought my grandmother was my mother and that I had the oldest mom in town."

"I know exactly what that's like," I lamented.

We talked for hours about the mistakes our parents made and how we'd be way smarter than them the day we had kids of our own, although we were speaking in general terms—Lisa hadn't even graduated from high school yet, and I sure as shit didn't have any intentions of becoming a father before I'd even reached eighteen.

"I saw you kissing that girl," Buddy told me one day, his shy eyes smiling. He liked to spy on me sometimes when I was coming back to the basement apartment.

"You did, huh?" I laughed. "Someday you'll have a girlfriend too. And you'll probably want to kiss her like I did."

He scrunched up his face. "No way! That's gross." He said it was gross, but I knew he just thought it looked funny.

"And when you meet that girl, you might even fall in love with her, marry her, and have babies someday," I joked.

Buddy's expression became gloomy. "I heard you tell her that you love her. Does that mean you don't love me and Mom and Dad anymore?" He stared at the ground timidly.

"No, of course not, Buddy. Why would you think that?" I crouched down to meet his downcast eyes. "You can love more than one person at once. I love you a lot and I always will. Just don't love more than one girlfriend at once, or you'll be in big trouble." I pinched his big cheeks and we laughed.

"Can we go outside and play together?" asked Buddy, raising his eyes to mine. There was so much in this apparently simple question.

"I can't right now. I have to go pick up Lisa. But I promise you this weekend we'll go outside and play."

He knew it wouldn't happen. What I saw wash over him in that moment made my heart tear. I'd let him down again. He just wanted to belong like I had so many years before, and I was making him feel like an outsider in my life.

In addition to being raised by our grandparents, Lisa and I were both smart, had a strong sense of responsibility, and were old for our years.

In Lisa, these traits led her to a realization that she wanted to become a schoolteacher. "I want to make a difference," she told me more than once. "You know, be there for kids. Help them learn and make good choices in life."

I encouraged her, ignoring the fact that I hadn't made time for my own kid brother, didn't trust teachers, and the choices I'd continued to make were anything but good in her book. But the world needed more people like her in schools. Her kind heart couldn't steer children wrong.

Even if she wasn't a racist or a fighter. In fact, she detested racism and violence of any sort. She wasn't crazy about the lyrics I wrote either. She didn't mind the music of WAY or any other white-power band that I listened to that much, but she refused to acknowledge the words at all. She did a good job of pretending the things she didn't like about me didn't exist. And somehow, they practically didn't when I was with her.

When Lisa and I were together, I didn't want to talk about ideology or revolution. It felt out of place. I wanted to discuss personal things, so I confided in her about my feelings of loneliness when I was younger, how I'd basically spent the first twelve years of my life drawing and daydreaming alone in my grandparents' coat closet; how I resented my parents for abandoning me for their jobs; how hard it was to straddle two completely different worlds like I had tried to do when I was bounced back and forth between Oak Forest and Blue Island.

Lisa found it odd that I had opted not to go to college. "You're so smart. What are you going to do with your life without a college degree?"

"I plan to start a business," I told her. "You can't learn what you need to know about being your own man in college. I've been figuring out ways to make things work since I was a little kid. I don't need a worthless piece of paper to prove that I can."

"You could get a degree in business, though."

"It's not my path."

"What is?"

"This is," I said, leaning in and kissing her tenderly on the lips.

We spent as much time as we could together. Day and night.

It didn't take me long to get comfortable with that. Aside from the joy of falling asleep with her in my arms and seeing her first thing every morning, it made all the other goals I'd set for myself seem trivial.

For the first time since my brother's birth, I felt totally aligned with one single person.

We built a world of two where nothing and nobody could reach us. Touching her cheek, feeling her hand in mine, her head on my shoulder, making love to her every night filled me with a sense of completeness and peace I'd never known. I knew her every look, knew what she was feeling before she verbalized it by catching the way her lip curled when she had something on her mind. No words were necessary to tell me what she was thinking.

And she knew me—my lonesomeness, my longing to leave my mark on the world. That was why, I think, she didn't try to stop my movement activities, even though she was wholly opposed to the racist world in which I was living. Lisa had been the ingredient to happiness I hadn't even known I was missing.

Shortly after Labor Day of 1991, Hector Diaz, the Anti who had falsely accused me of punching him, petitioned the court to have my suspended judgment revoked and the assault charge against me reinstated. He claimed I'd threatened him during my period of court supervision, which was no more true than the original accusation, though, similarly, it *was* something I might very credibly do.

Two Blue Island police officers took me into custody when I pulled into the EZ-Go gas station on Western Avenue to buy cigarettes. They towed my truck into the impound lot. I spent the night in the Blue Island lockup, next to a drunken vagrant who kept me awake all night snoring like a jackhammer, and I was released on my own recognizance at daybreak. Another court date was set.

I dressed respectfully again, acted polite and humble, bit my tongue until it bled, and clearly stated my innocence. The judge didn't believe me. Or maybe he did, but knew I was trouble and so decided to sentence me anyway.

It wasn't a harsh sentence, one hundred hours of community service, five days a week. I had to report to the Cook County courthouse at eight in the morning. Other people sentenced to community service would be there too, mainly for driving drunk, shoplifting, skipping out on child support, major traffic violations, etc. There were ten of us all together. We did janitorial work around the courthouse or were hauled off in a prisoner transport van with two county sheriffs to pick up garbage along the roadway or pull up weeds in empty city lots. We painted a couple of fences. I did this every weekday for a month for six to eight hours a pop to work off the time. I still went to work, making pizzas in the evening. I was concerned with how Lisa would take this brush with the law and was relieved that she took having an arch-criminal for a boyfriend in stride. She believed me when I had told her I hadn't done anything wrong, at least as far as threatening Hector Diaz.

ROCK-O-RAMA
Herbert Egoldt
5040 Brühl, Kaiserstr. 119
Tel. 02232/22584

011 49

MIT LUFTPOST
PAR AVION

MIT LUFTPOST
PAR AVION

W.A.Y.
Chris Picciolini
P.O. Box 734
... Ill. 60445

ROCK-O-RAMA
RECORDS

HERBE...
KAISERS...
D-5040 B...
TEL. 02...
POSTGIRO...
KÖLN 164...

IMPORT · HARDCORE · NEW WAVE · PUNK ·

W.A.Y.
Chris Picciolini
P.O.Box 734
Midlothian Ill. 60445
U.S.A.

DATUM

Hello Chris,

thank you for your letter + demo-tape.
Yes, if you like we would produce an lp with your band.
Please tell me any phone-no. I can get you.

Best regards,

17

HAPPY DEATH

I SPENT THE NEXT MONTH lining up interviews for WAY in a couple of skinhead newsletters, "zines" as we called them. The publications themselves were crude—badly made photocopies on poor-quality copiers, but that didn't matter. Skinheads were used to getting information that way and would read everything they could from the few printed things remotely resembling "racialist" literature.

When interviewed about who influenced me politically, I didn't hesitate to answer: the National Socialist German Workers' Party of the 1930s and contemporary English political organizations such as the National Front and Ian Stuart's Rock Against Communism. In America, we supported former KKK Grand Dragon and Republican Louisiana State Representative David Duke.

I answered questions about my views on specific subjects with earnestness, not remotely reluctant to have them known. *Blind Justice*, a British skinhead zine, had printed some of these views in its newsletter the previous year. At the top of the interview, an image of a Hitler Youth eagle with a swastika emblazoned on its breast and a sword and hammer clutched in its talons accented the page, wings spread wide open, ready for war. It was the perfect symbol for me, if not for everyone who supported WAY. Here's what I had to say in the article on various topics:

Gays: I think all queers should be sent to Mexico and blown to bits along with the Mexicans.

Jews: I despise Jews for one simple reason. They corrupt society with their evil lies. The Jewish parasites manipulate us and control our government, the banking system, and the media. I dislike Jews for the same reason that every civilization over the last three millennia has hated and banished them. They infect and kill every healthy thing they touch.

Race Mixing: I think race mixing is possibly the worst, most subhuman act against Mother Nature. We will soon see an end to this disease, because the Day of the Rope is returning.

Drugs: Drugs are for weak people who feel insecure about themselves; therefore they need the drugs to numb their feelings and enter an alternate reality. I am proud of who I am and don't need the false self-confidence that drugs provide.

Religion: I'm an agnostic and tend not to trust organized religions because they are as money-hungry as the Jews. If anything, I'd consider aligning myself with the Norse Odinist beliefs of warfare and reward. The principle of Victory or Valhalla resonates with me.

Zionism: The Zionist Jews stole the Holy Land, enslaved its people, slapped a Star of David on it and called it Israel. In spite of that, I'd be satisfied if every Jew just moved there and stayed out of America.

Capitalism: Capitalists can all rot in hell with their dirty blood money.

The press we'd been receiving put us in the movement spotlight overseas and in America, but it was just the tip of the iceberg.

Something much larger was brewing.

During my last week of community service for the phony Diaz beef, I assembled my WAY bandmates, and we cut a demo tape of six of our original songs. I had set up a microphone on a table during band rehearsal, and we had laid down a few tunes in one raw take.

The next morning I rushed to the post office and mailed copies to the famous French white-power record company Rebelles Européens and Rock-O-Rama Records, the legendary German label that handled all the prominent European skinhead bands, including Skrewdriver.

The French label offered us a record deal almost immediately, but I was gunning for Rock-O-Rama. So confident was I that when Gaël Bodilis, the owner of Rebelles Européens, called me from France to follow up on the offer he'd sent us in the mail, I politely turned him down without having heard from the other. And I neglected to inform my bandmates.

I tried following up by calling the Rock-O-Rama office in Germany repeatedly for the next two weeks to see if they'd received my package. After more than a dozen attempts, staying up late at night to call because of the seven-hour time difference, I finally got through and managed to talk to Herbert Egoldt, the owner of the record label. He was jovial and lighthearted and spoke to me with a crisp British accent. He said he'd received our tape and continued to utter the sweetest words I'd heard since Lisa first told me she loved me. He promised to fax over a recording contract within a few days. Luckily I'd lifted a fax machine a few weeks back from the driveway of a neighbor who was being evicted from his apartment.

The contract arrived as promised a few days later. In German. None of us in the band could follow a single foreign word of it, but what the fuck did we care? It meant we could make a record on the most prestigious skinhead label in the world. Exactly what I'd worked hard for. We had a deal on the table in early October, and I got the band to sign immediately on the dotted line and faxed it back.

Within a month, I arranged to record our first album in a studio called Square Bear Sounds in Alsip, a suburb just west of Blue Island. The owner, Stan Beringer, grew marijuana plants in the back room and was always high as a motherfucker. Although he looked like a mundane white stoner, he got a kick out of our blatantly racist music, even though he didn't seem to be particularly bigoted himself. He mainly recorded ghetto rap acts. I think he thought the band was an over-the-top gag, like a vulgar version of Weird Al Yankovic or something.

In the studio we cranked through track after track—thirteen in all—including a rousing rendition of Skrewdriver's signature anthem, "White Power," to close out the album. We altered the words slightly to make more geographic sense for our American and hometown Chicago fans.

White Power! Today.
White Power! For America.
White Power! For Chicago,
Before it gets too late.

As more "accomplished" musicians, Larry and Rick may have liked being in the studio, but I *loved* it. Despite the fixed pot stench in every piece of broken-down furniture and the lack of toilet paper in the grimy, roach-infested bathrooms, the process of recording all the different instruments onto separate tracks fascinated me. The whirring of the giant spinning reels of recording tape and the flapping sound when the tape hit the end of the spool was a joy to my ears. We were making magic.

Before we hit the studio, our bassist Davey had told us he was out. He had a real shot at becoming a professional skateboarder, and putting out a racist record would negatively influence his chances. We didn't want to hold him back, so we parted ways and brought in a replacement, Skinhead

Mark, to fill his role. Unfortunately, this didn't happen before Davey brought us a song that we inadvertently recorded and put on the record without knowing the main hook was lifted lick-for-lick from a New York City anti-racist hardcore band called Sick of It All.

Despite that, the mood in the studio was electrifying. Literally. Well into a long midnight session, while I was tracking my vocals I accidentally knocked over and spilled a beer on the recording booth floor, and trying not to interrupt our flow, as time and money were limited, I gripped the microphone and was instantly sent flying back against the wall. My steel-toed boot had been resting in the puddle of beer with a frayed cable when I gripped the shoddy microphone.

I didn't care. I would have died happy.

We recorded and mixed the entire album in five straight days for exactly $1,372, paid for by Rock-O-Rama Records. It was pressed first as a vinyl LP and later released as a compact disc when that format hit the mass market the following year. The album was officially listed as Rock-O-Rama release #123: White American Youth, *Walk Alone*. It was primarily sold in Europe, though a few record stores in Canada also carried it. But mainly, if you lived in the United States, you had to order it as an import by airmail and postal money order directly from the label in Germany. I was incredibly proud.

But it turned out to be a lousy deal for us. We didn't make a single dime and didn't even get a handful of free promotional records like bands typically do. Without knowing it, we'd essentially signed over one hundred percent of the rights to our recorded music in perpetuity to the label. Feeling both angry and foolish, I scraped up some cash and ordered fifty copies of the record at the wholesale price and sold them to our friends at cost to save face.

Everybody that mattered in Blue Island and the surrounding Chicago area knew we'd recorded the album. Even some of the Antis were surprisingly cool about it and defected to our side because of it. Despite the hodgepodge way Rock-O-Rama promoted their releases and managed the relationship with us, it didn't take long for the record to become popular among skinheads around the world. We officially joined the storied ranks of America's first crop of white-power bands. Along with Bound For Glory, Bully Boys, Arresting Officers, Max Resist & the Hooligans, and Midtown Bootboys, we were in good company. Exalted company, as far as I was concerned. Aside from WAY, Bound For Glory was the only other active American band on the legendary Rock-O-Rama roster.

Getting to play on a bill with Bound For Glory continued to be important to me. Hailing from the Twin Cities of Minnesota, they were the white-power musical outfit that had every American skinhead stomping their boots. Many had pegged them as the "Skrewdriver of the States," after Rock-O-Rama released their first album, *Warrior's Glory,* the previous year to critical movement acclaim. Their style was different than most of their British or American Oi! counterparts, bringing more homegrown thrash metal flavor to back up their pointed lyrics. Since they had quickly become the band everyone wanted to emulate and associate with, I made it a priority to get our bands to play together.

Not long after we released the *Walk Alone* album in early December of 1991, I was arrested yet again. To keep the movement alive—to make sure my name was seared into the brain of every youth in Blue Island—one of my associates showed up with me outside of Eisenhower one morning to protest in support of white students. We waved large signs emblazoned with "White Pride Worldwide," demanding "Equal Rights for Whites." I'd coordinated a dozen or so white students inside the school to join our demonstration by staging a cafeteria sit-in, refusing to go to class until school administrators agreed to grant them a white student union to rival the various minority student groups already in existence.

Car horns blared both approval and disdain. Passersby lobbed supportive shouts and disapproving projectiles at us. A news crew showed up. Cops came. The young protesters inside the school succumbed to the pressure of impending suspension and were shuffled back to class. Even though I never left the public sidewalk, I was arrested and charged with criminal trespassing on state property since I was no longer a student at the school. The previous restraining order against me didn't make it any easier. The protest made the local newspapers, and a Blue Island police detective identified me in an article as a "white supremacist mob boss."

"And proud of it," I would have added at the time if the reporter had interviewed me.

18

FINAL SOLUTION

FINALLY, AFTER MONTHS OF HARD WORK, we'd been booked to play in the same venue, on the same bill, as Bound For Glory, my favorite American white-power band. I'd corresponded with them some, but the interest was more on my part than theirs. WAY had been lined up to perform with them twice before, but skinhead concerts and fests were routinely shut down when some halfwit concert promoter would realize what kind of bands he'd actually booked.

Now, however, we were slated to play with Bound For Glory in Muskegon, Michigan. And not just in some basement or at some kegger party, we were confirmed to play in a real venue: the Ice Pick, a legit punk rock club.

On the day of the concert, the Ice Pick was overrun with at least three hundred white-power skinheads from around the Midwest and East Coast, a whole shitload of young hooligans full of rage and fury, waiting for an excuse to erupt into violence. The club was so packed I was surprised the fire marshal wasn't summoned to shut the show down. But nobody wanted to mess with this many of us.

I played it casual when I met Bound For Glory the first time, intent on not letting any traces of anxious energy show through.

White American Youth concert at the Ice Pick, Muskegon, Michigan, 1991

Despite my nerves, Big Ed Arthur, the guitarist and leader of Bound For Glory, and I hit it off immediately. It felt like we'd known each other for years. We became fast friends, connected by the fact that we were both first-generation Americans. His family had emigrated from Croatia around the same time mine had come over from Italy.

But as soon as WAY took the stage, one of the drunken East Coast skinheads in the crowd threw a beer can toward Rick, our guitarist, and accosted him for his long heavy-metal hair.

"Hippie scum," he babbled, headed for Rick, fists in the air. "I'll kick your dirty commie ass!"

Incensed anybody would go after Rick, I jumped in front of him, ready to beat this drunk asshole to a bloody pulp right there on stage for all to see.

Big Ed hopped up in a swift, sure move and wedged himself between us. His stare communicated to this dude so much more than what came out of his mouth. "They're with me."

The drunk backed down without hesitation and began apologizing. Everyone respected Big Ed. He was a massive, fully tattooed bear of a man. It was hard not to be intimidated by him. But all wasn't well. After our set was over, Rick was in a hurry to leave.

"This is crazy," he said. "That fucking guy wanted to kill me!" I tried to calm him down, but he was having none of it. Being a part-time racist, Rick wasn't used to the violence that came with the territory.

With Rick still stewing on our four-hour drive home from Michigan, things got worse when we stopped at a rest area to call home from a pay phone and received word that a mate from our crew, Jason Silva, had stabbed his girlfriend twenty-one times in an apparent lover's quarrel. We'd all been close friends with Jason and his girl. In fact, we often joked that all they did was argue like jealous lovers so they'd have an excuse to make up and fuck like wild rabbits.

Fucking Christ.

I felt sick about it, hoping that she'd pull through. She survived, but the horror of it was surreal. We were all speechless the rest of the drive home.

I knew this band couldn't hold together much longer. I had to assemble another one. And fast.

Meanwhile, my personal life couldn't have been going better. Even though high school took up Lisa's days, we spent our nights together. We never ran out of topics to discuss. I wanted to hear everything about her day. Nothing she said bored me. I kept most of my movement activities to myself, not wanting the ugliness that sometimes erupted to touch her. I shared the victories—progress with writing new songs, an interesting conversation I shared with somebody. But I never discussed the fights or the drama, and sure as hell never used the language with her that I used on the streets.

One night as I lay in bed watching her sleep, a profound sense of peace washed over me.

How could I be so fortunate? I loved everything about her—her innocence, her sincerity, her intellect, her loyalty, her kindness. We'd talked many times about spending the rest of our lives together. We both wanted children someday, and I loved that she could only imagine having them with me. I admired that she was passionate about helping kids, and I'd grown more comfortable with her plans to become a teacher. Maybe she'd find a way to change the system. Not all teachers had to push a false agenda. Lisa would be different. I was sure she was smart enough not to let college brainwash her.

As that thought hit me, a sharp realization accompanied it. If she were to go away to school, we would be apart. She would live in a world that didn't include me. It was a blow far more powerful than any I'd received in the countless fights I'd been in. It was unthinkable.

There was only one solution. I had to keep her here. I had to marry her.

I blocked out the voice condemning me for such a selfish act. I knew marriage might mean a major change in her plans for college, for her own future. I began planning my proposal. All worries about losing her faded as I began to visualize our lives together.

I bought her a chip of an engagement ring with what little money I had saved making pizzas, not at all certain how or where I'd ask her to marry me. She was still in her final year of high school. But I knew I couldn't wait until she graduated.

A multitude of scenarios passed through my head. The when and where of it. What I'd say. The expression on her face. Whether I'd be able to hold it together when I asked her.

The time came unexpectedly in December, just after my eighteenth birthday. Lisa and some of our mutual Beverly friends threw me a belated surprise birthday party, and as I was surrounded by people who cared for me and whom I cared for, people who thought enough of me to plan this whole special event, I knew the moment couldn't be more perfect.

In front of everyone, I held Lisa's hand, got down on one knee and declared, "I love you, Lisa. I can't imagine my life without you in it."

She was shocked, looking around at the equally surprised faces of our friends, not saying a word. Excited gasps became contagious in the room around us.

"Nobody makes me as happy as you do," I managed to say before getting choked up. I cleared my throat. "Will you allow me the honor of being your husband?"

She was taken aback. Sure, we'd spoken about marriage before, but never anything definite. We hadn't even been dating a year yet. Not even half a year. But she didn't hesitate. "Yes," she said, "yes!"

I took her gentle face in my hands and kissed her on the lips. The hushed silence in the room was shattered by cheers and beer bottles clinking. The girls in the room wiped their teary eyes.

I was eighteen. In love. And engaged to be married to a girl I cared deeply about.

I would make sure she never regretted joining her life with mine. Lisa would be proud to call herself my wife. I began to see my actions through that lens, and before long they appeared very different.

Through the movement grapevine, I heard Bound For Glory was heading overseas to Germany in March of '92 to play a concert. Doing so would make them the first white-power band from the United States to ever play a show on European soil. They'd make history.

I had to be part of this. It didn't matter to me that WAY had broken up when Larry and Rick left the group. I'd started a new band without missing a beat—Final Solution, in homage to the original band Clark, Carmine, and Chase Sargent had formed for a brief time in early 1985 at the genesis of the whole U.S. white-power skinhead movement. I had three months to prepare the band for our trip.

After some initial hesitation, I decided to write to Clark in prison about it. I asked his permission to resurrect the Final Solution name. Two years had passed since we'd corresponded and the materials that did still randomly trickle in from him bordered on nonsensical and repulsive. It had become clear to me that Clark was indeed seriously mentally ill. Relatively benign pornographic depictions of women had turned into sadistic, rambling tales of sexual violence and torture.

When a letter from Clark finally came back with his blessing on the use of the band name, I didn't respond to thank him. Thinking, even for a moment, how those sorts of twisted thoughts could enter someone's mind and escape their lips turned my stomach and made me feel dirty. I quickly put it behind me and moved forward.

This time every member of my band was a skinhead: two new guitarists, Mack and Hugo from the Indiana Hammerskin crew. Their friend Kenny Flanagan rounded out the group on drums. The only member of WAY that was part of my new band was Skinhead Mark, the bass player, whom we'd replaced Davey with a few months earlier when he'd bailed to follow his skateboarding dreams.

With some digging, I found out who was promoting the German concert. I phoned him late one night and said I'd performed with Bound For Glory previously in the States and insisted my new band travel with them to this concert as well. The promoter didn't put up any resistance whatsoever. He more or less said fine, if we could get there he'd let us co-headline the show.

So I called Big Ed from Bound For Glory and told him we'd be going along to Germany. They were getting paid to perform and set up with a place to stay. I let him know we'd fund our own trip and find our own place to bunk, but would be meeting them there. He seemed glad we were going.

I couldn't wait to tell Lisa the news. She'd go with me, of course. She'd spend her eighteenth birthday with me. I wanted to experience this milestone together, even if she'd want no part in the concert itself. She loved to take photographs and sketch architecture, and I thought we could travel together and split up when it was time to take care of band business.

The recruiting tactics for my Hammerskin chapter had shifted focus from printing and distributing flyers to strangers to producing music and using it as a targeted marketing tool to keep the flooding masses of new recruits—who were now coming in on their own volition—happy and engaged. As Final Solution's popularity gathered momentum, so did my recruiting efforts, and I was content simply conducting the chaos like a maestro leading a symphony. Earning a Hammerskin patch for their bomber jacket became an obsession for new probationary members, and I was the local gatekeeper. There were strict rules, like abstaining from drugs and respecting your brothers. I was satisfied with my position at the top of the Illinois Hammerskin pyramid, still leaving enough time for me to focus on the band and my beautiful fiancée.

A surprising thing about skinheads, though, was that for all the fear the media propagated, membership was actually relatively small compared to most American gangs. Across the nation, there were probably fewer than five thousand racist skinheads—of which only about five hundred were Hammerskins—yet we were considered a formidable force. From local cops to the FBI, law enforcement shuddered, thinking of what we might be up to or where we'd pop up next. People of color saw a kid with a shaved head, tattoos, and Doc Martens in their town and they were running to real estate agents and having earnest conversations about pulling their kids out of the local public school.

We had gotten the country's attention after Marty Cox called Oprah a monkey on national television, and we'd cemented the public's fear and loathing two years later when one of us busted Geraldo's nose on his talk show.

Every time a skinhead threw a punch or desecrated a synagogue, the media picked up on it and vilified us as violent right-wing extremists. So we didn't need a whole bunch of us to strike fear into the heart of America. Fifty of us partying together was reason enough to call in the SWAT team, the FBI, and the National Guard. As our numbers grew, so did our terroristic behavior.

During the stifling summer of 1990, two Houston, Texas, skinheads stomped a fifteen-year-old refugee from Vietnam to death. According to one of the killers, the kid's last words were, "God forgive me for coming to this country. I'm so sorry."

The following year, some other Texas Hammerskins murdered a black man who had been seen hanging out with white people, in a drive-by shooting. A few months later, Aryan National Front skinheads from Birmingham, Alabama, beat a homeless black man to death on Christmas Eve. Shortly after, four other skinheads stabbed and killed another transient.

While our numbers weren't big, white-power skinheads were spread out far and wide and tucked into every corner of the country. We took turns hosting rallies and fests to bring our loose network together and exchange information. Though people might not otherwise travel a long distance for a meeting, when we added old friends, aggressive white-power music, and beer to the agenda, it was a guarantee skinhead guys and gals would drive hundreds of miles to get drunk with their friends and hear music from the few bands singing their tunes.

Skinhead gatherings were like white-supremacist pep rallies. The energy at these events reignited our weary fires. It gave others who came solely to experience the music another chance to join our intrepid efforts to save the white race. It's pretty damn hard to listen to hours and hours of aggressive music preaching about the need to fight those trying to destroy the people you love and not to come away pissed off, ready to do something about it.

Music was usually preceded by fiery speakers. Sometimes I was one of them. We'd get up on stage and set the tone through communicating that our nation was in jeopardy. "Heil Hitler," we'd say.

Hands would shoot up with the precision of a well-trained Nazi brigade. "Heil Hitler," the devotees would shout back.

"Our goal today is simple. We're here to listen to a little white-power music."

Whistles, cheers. Stiff-armed salutes from those who weren't double-fisting cans of cheap beer.

"And we're here to secure the existence of our race and a future for white children!"

The response was invariably deafening.

"I'll bet you know there are people who don't want us here today. Who tried to stop this peaceful gathering."

More cheers and boot stomping.

"But they can't stop us," the speaker would scream into the microphone. "It is our God-given birthright to assemble here and exercise our right to speak freely. The meddling Jews who run this country and own the media would love nothing more than to shut us up because they know we're on to their secret ZOG scheme to destroy our proud European culture. They know we've got their number. We have got the guts and the motive to hunt them down and take them out.

"The niggers are right alongside them, and they won't be happy until they see *us* in chains. If we'd run them out of our country and back to Africa like we should have when slavery was abolished, or strung them all up by their filthy necks from the nearest bridges, they wouldn't be here now to pollute our cities and sell their poison to innocent white kids. They wouldn't be raping our women and living off our hard-earned wages."

By that point, it didn't even matter what the firebrand had to say. The crowd would be going wild, the words lost in the fervor and inebriation. Ready for the music.

The band would start, its guitars deafening, drums pounding, nefarious words of faith spewing into the microphone.

Glory be to the white man and woman.

By the end of the show, fights would break out all over the place: the Atlantic City skins against the crew from Philly; the old-school skinheads feuding with overzealous fresh-cuts. And with an overwhelming ratio of men to women in the movement, you could be sure someone would try to screw your girlfriend too, and a bloody brawl would ensue.

While things in Blue Island couldn't have been going better for me and my crew, I began to have nagging worries—the first rational thoughts I'd allowed myself in years—regarding others within the movement. I worried over how the flawed gamecock mentality, the inherent aggression that skinheads expressed against even their own kind, so often presented itself at these gatherings and didn't mesh well with my own sensibilities. Unity and respect were paramount back home. Friends helped each other and didn't dare cross one another. There was a sense of loyalty to your team. From the CASH skins to my Eisenhower teammates and even the High Street Boys, we relied on that special bond to move us forward. I feared that outside our own Chicago bubble, such cooperation might be impossible, and our movement could be subsumed with infighting. I found it harder and harder to convince myself that most of the people I'd met over the years weren't ignorant, white-trash thugs. They weren't interested in saving the white race as much as guzzling their courage and vomiting words they could never back up without a pack of bloodthirsty attack dogs at their side to overcompensate for their own lack of nerve. Stupidity and alcohol inevitably burst into a flash of skinhead fists and fury.

I'd stand back and watch, more and more often disgusted. How the hell were we going to reclaim glory for the white race when we couldn't even protect ourselves from our own petty insecurities? It was going to be an uphill battle.

I was willing to bet our European comrades had it more together. For one thing, Europe was where the whole skinhead movement had begun in the sixties, and they had decades of experience on their side. The time had come for their American counterparts to operate at the same level. I decided I'd soak in what could be learned from them on my trip to Germany. By the time I'd cemented our appearance overseas, Final Solution had already built a decent fan base there. We'd already performed all over our own country—Georgia, Tennessee, Michigan, Minnesota, Illinois, Indiana—at rallies with more than five hundred skins and Nazis, a large number in terms of attendance at skinhead concerts in the U.S., and enough that it inevitably spooked everybody in town who were at all unsure what we were about. It was a guarantee that wherever we played, you'd find FBI and local law enforcement there taking snapshots of the attendees and adding more info to their already overstuffed files.

One of the more hilarious instances of police harassment occurred when I was pulled over by a state trooper while driving home from a get-together in Atlanta, Georgia. Upon searching my vehicle, behind my driver's seat, the officer uncovered a wooden coffee table leg with a long, pointy lag bolt sticking out horizontally from its end.

"What's this for, son? Do you intend to use this as a weapon for your Aryan revolution?"

"No, sir, officer," I replied. "I intend to add it to my three-legged coffee table as soon as I get home. I'm getting tired of it tipping over every time I put my copy of *Mein Kampf* on it." Even he couldn't help but laugh at that.

We performed in all types of venues: warehouses, anybody's private property where we could throw up a makeshift stage and plug our gear into a gas generator. The Detroit Hammerskins had their own private social club and charged five bucks to get in. We played on their stage a number of times. It was always a good party—until the drunken hypocrites started fighting again.

Climbing the rungs of the American white-power ladder felt as natural as sacking a quarterback or punching someone in the face. And with it came applause, respect, and admiration.

My lonely life and fractured childhood identity were things of the past. I now had a beautiful fiancée, hundreds of loyal associates, a band about to make history, and I was headed to the land of Adolf Hitler and our National Socialist predecessors to loudly profess my faith and once again march victoriously through their streets.

Could life possibly get any better than this?

19

OPEN YOUR EYES

Weimar, Germany, was a place I knew little about. I had no idea the famous writers Johann Wolfgang von Goethe and Friedrich Schiller had lived there, not a clue that one of history's greatest pianists, Franz Liszt, had spent part of his life in the city. I didn't know philosopher Johann Herder had called it home or that Friedrich Nietzsche lived out the final years of his life there. I didn't even know that artist Paul Klee, whom the Nazi party had denounced for creating "degenerate" art, had been a resident of this eastern German town.

Nor did I know that the Nazis had set up a concentration camp nearby—Buchenwald. More than fifty thousand political prisoners, including Jews, gays, Catholics, criminals, and children, met their deaths in this camp. Conditions were said to be so horrendous that many died of typhoid and starvation. Others were shot in the back of the head. Thousands of people were slaughtered by lethal injections, and countless others were victims of inhumane medical experiments that included the use of the deadly Zyklon B gas. The camp displayed the tattooed human skin of murdered prisoners as "modern art" in an area called the "pathological block." But even though I didn't know a damned thing about Weimar, I knew that Adolf Hitler was a leader I admired.

Final Solution, Weimar, Germany, 1992

When we arrived, I paid little attention to the people or history of the town. I was oblivious to the fact that in this city of little more than sixty thousand people, there were twenty museums full of art, literature, and music. What did I care? What the hell did the past have to do with me? All that mattered to me was that white skinhead warriors from all over Europe were getting together for one epic concert in Germany, Hitler's stomping ground—and that I was going to play a memorable part in this historic event.

Despite the swelling support from the thousands in attendance, I felt lonely. I'd be the only remaining original skinhead from back home in Blue Island who'd made it this far, who'd embraced the lasting legacy we created and fought so hard for. Carmine Paterno and Chase Sargent had drifted away. The Manson girls had moved on, likely to idolize some other burgeoning charismatic sociopath. The superfluous few had vanished. And Clark Martell had lost his mind.

But I'd forged ahead, still inspired by the first words of Clark I'd ever read:

> *We must throw ourselves, blood, bone, sinew, and soul, behind the skinhead battering ram as it rolls with the splitting of wood through the gates of power into the evil one's domain, now ours to reclaim, with the skinhead anthem upon our tongues and the flag in our hearts.*

The Weimar concert ended up being everything I imagined. Four thousand racial brothers and sisters—assembled from all over Europe—effectively invaded the quaint German burg. Every beer hall, restaurant, and cobblestone street was inundated with white soldiers from far and wide, as if 1930s Nazi Germany had squeezed through a wrinkle in time to the present day. It was the first time an American white-power band stepped foot on European soil to play a concert, and rumors flourished that Ian Stuart might even attend and perform some acoustic songs.

Lisa had stayed behind at the hostel in Munich to wander around and take photographs of the architecture. I'd catch up with her as soon as the concert ended. But for now, my mind was focused on the performance ahead.

We were second to last on stage that evening—preceded by the most popular German skinhead bands like Radikahl, Märtyrer, Kraftschlag, and Störkraft—and the crowd was ready to absorb some truth. When our time came, I grabbed the microphone and didn't waste time on small talk. As soon as our instruments were tuned, our equipment turned on, guitars plugged in, I motioned for the band to start.

Ear-splitting, pounding beats filled the walls of the once-upon-a-time hallowed church faster than a candle could be lit in effigy for our sins. Or blown out. Any holy souls still lingering among the memories of mass and Christ sensed hell was upon them as my voice echoed through the loudspeakers:

Clear the streets, the SS marches.
It's time for white revolution.
What do we want? Six million Jews!
Another final solution.
Sieg heil!

The applause began midway through our first song and never died down.

At last, I was the hero of the football team being carried off on the shoulders of my squad, the fans drunk with appreciation. If I had lingering doubts about my message, about the skinhead scene, if I had reservations about the white race's superiority—or if what I was doing was right—at that moment I didn't care. This was what I had been born for.

"Heil Hitler!" I shouted.

The crowd was out of its mind around me. Four thousand skinheads were on their feet, boots stomping, arms outstretched in glorious salute, beams of sharp-edged white light washing over shaved heads, sweat breaking over swastika tattoos black as sin, awash in pulsating strobes.

No one seems to understand why I'm fighting.
Can't you see we've got to even the score?
Why won't you open your eyes? Why won't you open your eyes?

Me on stage, leading it all.

The afternoon following the concert, I traded goodbyes with my band in Weimar and boarded a train to meet up with Lisa in Munich, the city where we'd started our European journey together.

By the time I arrived, I was exhausted. I could see her from across the train platform, searching for me in the distance. The moon's silvery glow cast an iridescent outline around her body. It was dark, but I could see the soft silhouette of her face. I approached quickly, and as I got closer, she turned and opened her arms to embrace me.

Her eyes were gentle, comforting. Her hand reached to caress my cheek, and I pulled her in close, lifting her to her toes and giving her a passionate kiss.

After spending a glorious few days with Lisa picnicking on hillsides and visiting museums and parks around Munich that she'd discovered before I'd arrived, I left her once again and took a standing-room-only overnight train alone to Cologne. I showed up without an appointment to

Rock-O-Rama headquarters in Brühl, where I dropped in unannounced on owner Herbert Egoldt, a round, old man whom I quickly realized wasn't even a racist. It seemed he didn't give a damn about much of anything but making money. He was a capitalist, pure and simple.

As he led me into his office, I met his shallow eyes with a steely stare, letting him know I was on to him. He'd pay my band album sales royalties, never mind that Rock-O-Rama was widely known as a non-paying label. I'd make sure and lead the way for him to start paying the bands he'd fleeced for years. Not for a lack of trying, I never got a dime from Herbert or the label. His burly warehouse goons made sure of that. But I did manage to leave with a small box of about thirty various white-power CDs.

After spending only an hour at the office, I took a taxi back to the train station and headed back to Munich to spend my final days with Lisa.

The high from the trip lingered once we got back home, but daily life immediately interfered with my renewed commitment to fight for the white race. I'd had a taste of the ultimate form of acceptance: adoration.

So what the hell was I doing still working in a pizza place? I wondered. I was better than that.

Something had to give—I needed a better job. A persistent voice inside me began to wish I'd taken formal education more seriously. But I shut that voice down and used my lack of decent-paying employment opportunities to my advantage. I spoke to my recruits with great fervor about the work ethic, the importance of providing for our loved ones, and I ranted against anyone I could blame for making it impossible for good, clear-thinking, hardworking white Americans to put food on their tables and feed their families.

"There is honor working in factories, making goods for our fellow whites," I said to anyone who would listen. "There is no shame in driving trucks and getting these American-made goods from local factories to stores owned and operated by white moms and pops who know what they want, who understand their needs. And at the end of the week, after paying the bills through our sweat and labor, it's good to relax and enjoy ourselves like we're doing here together now, among our own folk.

"We don't need any capitalists peddling their multiracial degeneracy to our children. We don't need more criminals from third-world countries flooding in and taking what few scraps we have left away from us. What we need to do is prepare ourselves for war. To be the righteous freedom fighters that our destiny demands us to be in this struggle to reclaim our American rights!"

I made it a point to attend every rally I could, no matter how small. I performed music, keeping the energy flowing as younger skinhead candidates joined us. But I took a less active role in any confrontations. I'd already seen my fair share of combat. I'd made a name for myself. I had nothing left to prove. It was time for somebody else to deal with the cops and bruises. That's what soldiers were for. And by this time, I had an abundance of them ready to obey my every order.

I was firm, but I was a fair commander. I taught my recruits how to respect themselves, though woefully missing was any lesson on how to respect the "other." Many of them had been marginalized or lonely kids with low self-esteem, traumatized, desperately searching for acceptance. The traits that made them loathe themselves made them easy targets and gave me a reason to save them—they'd do anything they were told in order to have something to belong to and an existence other than the miserable one they left behind. And if they got arrested for carrying out a mission or if they got hurt, there were others ready to step out of the shadows to take their places and pledge their support.

Meanwhile, my love for Lisa kept growing, and when she told me three months later that she was expecting our child, I was overjoyed.

"I'm pregnant," she cried.

"We're going to have a baby, Lisa? That's amazing!"

She sobbed. What about her plans? What about college? What about becoming a teacher? Needing comfort and reassurance, I took her gently into my arms.

I am ashamed to say that part of my happiness over the pregnancy was that it meant she would stay with me. She wouldn't be going off to college, making new friends, having a new life I wasn't a part of. I held her tight and tenderly kissed her tears away. "This is wonderful. What we've wanted all along. Maybe it's earlier than we planned, but that doesn't matter. We are going to bring a child, our child, into the world. And we won't be like our parents. We'll do this right. It's fate that we have this child now."

I nestled Lisa close, stuffing her fears away. "I love you, and I love this baby," I said, assuring her that everything would be okay.

My mother was not pleased.

I hadn't been sure how to tell her, only that I needed to do so immediately. I still technically lived under my parents' roof, and I might need their help financially until I found a better-paying job. While she didn't spend too much time in church, my mom still considered herself a devout Catholic, and a child born out of wedlock was a mortal sin to her. Besides, what Italian mother would raise a boy to have a child before he was married? Nonno and Nonna would be disappointed.

I tried easing my mother into the idea. Lisa and I clearly needed to live together now. I said it was my duty to help provide for our child.

I don't know which came faster, her tears or the throwing of her shoes at me from across the room. "What have you done? You're only a child yourself! You aren't a man yet, and she's still a schoolgirl." My father had left the room without saying a word.

I waited patiently, letting her get it all out.

But then she said something I hadn't expected. "This can be fixed," she declared, eyes wild as a loon's, wiping away her tears. "She can have an abortion."

Rage filled my veins, and I rose like a dust storm, swept over to her. "How dare you suggest something like that to me. You think I should destroy my own child? If you ever say anything like that again, even so much as think it, you will never meet your grandchild. And you'll never see me again."

I left the room, seething.

My mother came around—she always did—and by the time Lisa graduated from school and our wedding in June of 1992 approached, my mother had become proud of the fact that not only would she have a daughter-in-law, but she would also soon be a grandmother.

Our wedding was intimate, held in a quiet, non-denominational ceremony in a quaint little chapel in the woods.

Thirty people attended—Lisa's family, my parents and grandparents. The groomsmen—my bandmates from Final Solution—all had their heads freshly shaved and their muttonchop sideburns aptly trimmed for the occasion. They shined their boots to wear with their black tuxes. The contrast between them and Lisa's bridesmaids—all girlfriends of hers from her Catholic high school—was something to behold.

Buddy was a stout little ring bearer in his mini tuxedo, as he led my bride through the chapel doors and down the aisle. Lisa's emerald eyes glimmered as she passed through the shafts of sunlight beaming through the narrow, rose-hued chapel windows. When her gaze lifted and caught mine, time paused in a moment of suspended reality. Kubiak—my best man—snuck a flask of whiskey from his jacket pocket and passed it along to the other groomsmen. But if the wedding was small, the reception more than made up for it. My parents wouldn't allow Lisa and me to have the small gathering we wanted for fear the other Italians would badmouth them as cheapskates, so they sprung for a large Italian affair with more than two hundred guests. We had relatives from both sides, skinheads, and Catholic school girls, all eating and drinking together and having a grand time. Traditional Italian tarantellas rang out, interspersed with punk rock ballads my drunken mates strong-armed the wedding deejay to play. The Bound For Glory guys, who had their own table, hit the dance floor when it came time for the garter tossing. It was practically a case study on how mixing people with different backgrounds creates a more vibrant environment, and in retrospect I don't know how I was able to overlook that.

Of course, the cops patrolled the parking lot of our reception. They'd been told I was getting married and wanted to document who showed up. I was so happy that it didn't get to me. I even brought some cake out to their unmarked cars.

While our honeymoon was short—I couldn't get time off work—and the location less than romantic—we stayed at Lisa's grandparents' mobile home on a small lake in rural Michigan—we couldn't have been happier.

I carried my beautiful bride across the trailer's threshold and set her down on the sofa bed. In typical Italian fashion, we'd been given stacks of cash as gifts by our wedding guests. We sat on the bed and counted it. Fourteen grand! We were rich.

We threw it in the air, watching it drift back onto us.

We were going to start our lives out right, the happiest couple alive.

20

AMERIKKA

I SETTLED INTO MARRIED LIFE EFFORTLESSLY. I was bringing in a steady if meager salary, working full-time at the pizza place. And Lisa had begun working part-time at a furniture store in town. With some semblance of financial stability, and figuring my mother could help with the baby, Lisa and I rented the smaller of the second-floor apartments in my parents' two-story building.

Like all couples in love for the first time, we believed our bond was stronger and more special than anything anyone had ever known.

Soon, however, I realized I wasn't earning enough to afford my growing family and the lifestyle I wanted. It was time to look for a real job.

I eventually found work on a road construction crew, with a company making and distributing road barricades and doing traffic control—setting highway lane closures, detours in construction zones.

When I started the job, I made a little over four bucks an hour, but with overtime, I knew I could bring home more than minimum wage. The job suited my distorted identity and ego—what could be a nobler way to prove myself as a hardworking white man than joining the working-class stiffs doing manual labor?

After about six months of assembling road construction signs and traffic barricades in a warehouse and loading them on trucks, one of the foremen said I was a hard worker, so he would let me go out on the road to assist one of the drivers with setting lane closures. I'd pull the flashing traffic horses off the truck and set them in place to close lanes and detour traffic.

Before long my boss made me the permanent road assistant for a shift supervisor on a long-term highway resurfacing project in the city. This meant putting in long days, but I didn't complain. Even though I'd become increasingly distant from my Chicago crew since I found out Lisa was pregnant, I knew the job would allow me to lead by example, that I could both work hard and propagandize those I came into contact with here the same way I had done everywhere else.

While I didn't advertise my skinhead activities on the job, I didn't hide them either. My work boots were steel-toed Doc Martens, my growing number of racist tattoos clearly visible on my arms. Coincidentally, I wasn't the only white supremacist around. Bernie Johansson—a rotund older gentleman with an unwieldy salt-and-pepper handlebar mustache—had worked for the company for thirty years and made no secret of his long-standing membership in the American Nazi Party. He would sit in the warehouse break room openly reading movement literature and wearing white-power T-shirts under his paint-spattered overalls. We hit it off immediately. He gave me stacks of new books to read, and even though I knew most of the content already—I had read the same arguments a thousand times—I devoured them during work breaks.

Whenever I could spare the time off from work and Lisa was busy with her job, I still traveled and performed at rallies out of state and spoke vehemently about my beliefs. Lisa wanted nothing to do with my racist rantings, nor did I want her or the child we would have to be any part of the hostility that surged through the gatherings. I had begun to recognize that a paradox existed in the white-power movement—a movement dominated by insecure men—where outwardly we'd praise white women as goddesses and the progenitors of our great warrior breed, but the truth was that in closed quarters the women were often treated worse than the people we claimed to hate. Most believed that women's sole purpose was to pop out Aryan babies and fetch cold beer. But in my blind ambivalence, I somehow convinced myself that I was a different kind of hero, wading neck-deep through that mire, carrying a family that I loved on my shoulders so they could benefit from my sacrifice.

I continued to spread my own brand of vitriol with a vengeance, while I gave my wife puppy-dog eyes full of love and put my head to her stomach and whispered lullabies to our unborn child, and the two of us giggled when he kicked so hard we could see her stomach move. By all appearances, I was still a committed violent extremist intent on doing damage to anyone unlike us.

In September of 1992, two months before our child was born, I headed to Pulaski, Tennessee, to attend the Aryan Unity March, a rally held by the Fraternal Order of White Knights of the Ku Klux Klan. The location was significant—the original KKK had been founded in Pulaski on Christmas Eve in 1865.

It wasn't my first Klan rally, but it was a rare opportunity for me to spend time with many of the skinheads and fellow white supremacists I'd known and been corresponding with from around North America. At the birthplace of the Ku Klux Klan I'd represent Blue Island, the birthplace of the American neo-Nazi skinhead movement.

The day of the rally was hot, the smell of steamy asphalt hanging in the thick, musty air like the hordes of law enforcement officers littering the rooftops of the town.

I was dressed for combat: my fourteen-eyelet black Doc Martens shone slick and my jeans rolled up so the blood that was sure to flow through the streets would not stain them. My head was shaved to a close crop, and I took the thin black suspenders off my shoulders. They hung at my sides, a statement to my enemies that I was ready to fight and defend my race with my sweaty, balled-up fists. The boots were heavy on my feet, and sweat rolled down my back. The humidity was dangerous, and so was the tension in the air. Feds were not so subtly stationed all over the streets, taking our photos with cameras bearing lenses as long as their arms.

Hundreds of skinheads, people dressed in Klan robes and Nazi regalia, and racists of a more general ilk congregated at the designated staging area. Men with bullhorns barked orders for us to come together and shouted motivational white-power cheers, which were followed by stiff-armed salutes.

The air was thick with banners—Confederate flags, Nazi battle flags, hand-painted placards with sayings like "God Hates Niggers," "Join The KKK," and "Save the White Race. Unite!"

The attacks of September 11, 2001, hadn't happened yet, but with the American white-power movement in full swing, most Americans were living in fear of every move we made. As far as mainstream America was concerned, we were the most dangerous extremists within our borders. And the truth was, they were right.

The lust for blood was palpable. There were among us militiamen in camouflage with riot helmets and Nazi armbands.

As rebel flags and swastikas cut furiously through the air, so did the chants and protests from hundreds of people who had gathered to oppose us. Black and white, old and young, male and female, they were united by their commitment to stop us from marching. They were clamoring for us, only held back by a thin blue line of Pulaski policeman and Tennessee state troopers.

The mob of counter-demonstrators grew by the second, and they were loud, far louder than we were, even with our bullhorns.

They held up peace fingers, and we flipped them off, taunting them with racist epithets and a barrage of "die, race traitor" and "faggot cocksucker" obscenities.

They carried signs demanding world peace.

We thought we carried the weight of the world.

That's when it dawned on me: I ached for Lisa more than anything, more than I wanted a white homeland even. For a brief moment I became lost in scanning the faces of some of the counter-protestors. I felt for the first time as if I were coming face to face with some of the people from my past. There was the gay brother one of my friends had, who was always interesting and funny and kept mostly to himself. And my black teammates from my Eisenhower football team who had never given me trouble despite the horrible things I said about them and the violence I facilitated. The thoughts and words from the last five years of my life were taking on new resonance in my head—as if I were hearing things I'd said played back to me, and they sounded like they were in someone else's voice.

Why was I here and not at home with my pregnant wife whom I adored, with my hand on her belly, taking in every moment with her? I suddenly felt guilty and out of sorts. I didn't respect these people, the Klansmen, the racist clergyman wearing a priest's collar around his neck and a KKK patch over his heart, the mother carrying her infant with a tiny Klan hood on, the inbred hick with missing teeth and a beer-stained "Niggers Suck" T-shirt.

There were fellow skinheads here too, "brothers" and "sisters" whom I related to from neighborhoods like I came from, urban jungles, rather than Southern swamps. But even with them, I was starting to question what this struggle was about.

It was about pride, I rationalized, being proud of our white heritage and standing up against those who wanted to take that away from us. My thoughts drifted back to my earliest memory of holding Lisa in my arms, her pleading eyes searching deep inside me for my truth. "Why do you have so much hate inside of you?" she'd questioned. "You're so caring and gentle to me sometimes. Which one is the real you?" Suddenly I wasn't so sure.

Ahead of me, the Grand Dragon of the prevailing KKK faction within our group proclaimed this was once again the birthplace of a white revolution. Niggers, queers, and Jews were the enemy.

I knew all that—niggers were raping our women and forcing drugs on our youth. It didn't happen in my town, but presumably it was more prevalent in theirs. Jews controlled our lives, and queers destroyed white propagation. And somehow—choose the reasoning you like—the fact that we never saw evidence of these claims was itself evidence of their existence. That was how good the Jews and their secret plan for a "New World Order" were at obscuring their crimes.

I saw that the peace-loving protesters, gathered by the hundreds, waving peace flags and holding hands singing folk songs, had resorted to ripping up chunks of concrete from the sidewalk to violently pelt us with.

We inspired so much animosity in those who believed in only peace that they were trying to hurt us with violence.

The Nazi salutes had tired my arm, and the cries for white power had strained my voice.

When the march came to an end and my comrades were celebrating by getting hammered with booze, I was hit by the disturbing thought: how would I know if this whole thing was simply an endless cycle of excuses to fight and drink and commiserate? To belong to an exclusive club of other people more fucked up than you?

I felt stuck in a hole too deep to climb out of. The life of a violent white supremacist was all I'd known through nearly every single one of my teen years. Who would I be otherwise? Where would I go?

Confusion overwhelmed me, and I felt as if someone had landed a solid blow to my solar plexus. Along with my breath, my commitment was knocked out of me for the first time, and for a brief moment I clearly saw there was a serious problem with my reality.

I returned home ready to try harder than ever to prove my worth as a man. I threw myself wholeheartedly into my construction job. The hours were long, the work at times grueling and other times mind-numbingly inane, but we needed the money. Aside from the wedding cash, which we'd earmarked to use as a down payment to buy a home, we were broke and expecting a child in two months.

We lived on forty-nine-cent packages of ramen noodles and macaroni and cheese. I had no health insurance at work, so Lisa was on public aid for her prenatal care. I didn't let myself dwell on the fact that I was dependent on taxpayers' money to bring my child safely into the world, something I had criticized minorities for "exploiting" hundreds of times over the last few years.

I did far more than my share of work. Putting in sixteen-hour days was normal. Sometimes I worked even more hours than that. In fact, the night Lisa went into labor, I'd just come off an eighteen-hour shift.

Then, just as quickly, that clarity faded. I was far too worn out to be the overanxious dad on the way to the hospital, but I came alive when I got into the delivery room. I watched Lisa's every anguished expression intently. Labor was long, and every hour on the hour nuns came on the hospital's loudspeaker to read verses from the New Testament. It drove us nuts, but being on public assistance we were in no bargaining position—this was the hospital we'd been assigned to by the welfare agency.

After an eternity or two, our son Devin was born.

He was not much bigger than my own two worn and battered hands—hands that had been curled into vengeful fists since I was a child—and as

I cradled him in my lap for the first time, I promised him I would be the best father in the world, no matter what it took.

Lisa squeezed my hand.

Caressed by the soft, gentle breath of our fragile son, I was carried away momentarily from the uncertain reality of being a nineteen-year-old father shouldering the vestiges of a fraying cause. My child's sweet, precious scent filled my lungs. I inhaled deeply and felt it permeate my soul.

My son's life was in my hands, both literally and figuratively, and never had I been charged with a greater purpose.

For the first time in my adult life, I broke down and wept.

21

SOLDIERS OF THE RACE WAR

THE BIRTH OF OUR SON CHANGED MY LIFE. I started to imagine the world through his eyes, still unsullied by any prejudice. Babies know nothing of differences—the color of someone's skin is meaningless to them; they have no concern for someone else's beliefs, net worth, or sexual identity. The only thing that seemed to matter to Devin was love, and he could cry until he was embraced by it.

If I could have held on to that sense of clarity, that love more pure than I could have imagined that surged through me when I looked into his eyes, if I could have honored that feeling in my every act and deed from that moment on, tragedy may well have been prevented.

But I was young, and careless in ways that horrify me still. Instead of respecting the power of love my son had brought into my life, I let my signals get crossed, and I convinced myself more than ever that I had to make the world safe for my child by protecting him from the dangers I still believed existed, even if they seemed irrelevant in my newborn son's eyes—blacks, Jews, gays—anybody who wasn't white and proud, who came from a culture I refused to understand, whom I still feared as a potential threat.

For a few weeks after the Pulaski KKK march, I could sense the hate in me starting to dissolve as I viewed my life through a new perspective,

Christian and Devin Picciolini, 1993

but then it was as if my worst impulses rebelled, afraid of the revelations that were starting to occur to me. My mission to protect my race and ensure a safe existence for my child became even more critical.

Lisa and I decided it was time to buy our own home. We found a modest, two-bedroom duplex that suited us, used the money we'd received from our wedding as a down payment, and moved in shortly after Devin was born. My parents said they were proud of me. Finally. Here was their nineteen-year-old son with a good job, his own home, and a family. What a good boy. My grandparents were pleased with me too. Only nine-year-old Buddy could recognize the irredeemable selfishness that ruled my life. "You hardly ever do anything with me, and you're living in the same building," he said. "Now that you're leaving I'll never see you."

"Sure you will," I promised. "I'll be over here all the time to visit with the baby."

He pushed me away and thumped his little fist down on the kitchen table. I'd never seen him upset like this. "You just love the baby. You don't love me anymore." The words crushed me. Based on the way I had abandoned Buddy, I understood full well why he felt that way.

"Buddy," I pleaded. "How can you say that? *Of course* I love you."

He ran to his bedroom and slammed the door so hard that a framed picture of the Roman Colosseum hanging in hallway slid to the floor and shattered. "Buddy?" I knocked gently. "Buddy, please open up."

"Go away! Leave me alone." I'd heard that before, but it had been from my own lips.

I'd watched my shy and innocent little brother grow up from a distance. And only now had his resentment of me become fully visible through my own self-imposed fog.

But Buddy was no longer the wide-eyed pudgy nuisance that I once so easily brushed away. Now I could hear in his voice the loneliness, the anger that had started to take over my thoughts at his age, the wanting desperately for someone to pay attention. And for good reason that warning sign was something hard to ignore.

I continued to coordinate the Chicago Hammerskins—albeit from a more remote position than I had in the past—while I dutifully worked my construction job six or seven days a week.

During every Chicago winter, my construction group continued to temporarily disband, and the months between paychecks were becoming a problem. It had been tough enough living on unemployment wages for four months every year when there were only two of us to support. With an infant, that was virtually impossible. It didn't take me long to figure out I could supplement my unemployment checks by importing and selling music on the side to my growing network of white supremacists. White-power music was extremely difficult to come by—record stores would not sell it—so most people who listened to it would settle for third-generation audio dubs of whatever they could find within their circle of friends.

I recognized that the opportunity to buy wholesale and save money on shipping and taxes existed if I was able to place larger orders, so I revived my relationship with Rock-O-Rama in Germany and bought a handful of popular titles from them and marked up the prices a few dollars. I began peddling a variety of white-power albums—old and new—so I always had something fresh to sell.

It seemed like a golden opportunity to work on two of my commitments at once—I brought in an extra two hundred dollars a week for my family by selling music while I was laid off from my job, and I was able to keep promoting my ideology. For once, the two worlds seemed to blend together.

In the spring of 1993, HBO aired *Skinheads USA: Soldiers of the Race War*, a documentary about a group of young white-power skinheads living in the South. The film opened with a scene showing my band Final Solution performing live during a celebration commemorating Hitler's birthday at the Aryan Youth Front compound in Alabama, a rocky plot of land owned and run by an older Nazi named Will Manfredi, whom I'd never met. I figured it would be amazing exposure for the movement, even though the film focused on the movement's incredible hatred and its wild contradictions and depicted skinheads as a bunch of depraved lunatics.

It turned out that footage was from the band's final show. Skinheads from all over the United States were set to travel to the Aryan Youth Front gathering, and we'd been asked to perform at the last minute when it dawned on the organizers that there wasn't enough planned in the way of entertainment. I didn't hesitate. Our band had been slowly coming apart with my new commitments forcing me to realize I couldn't keep it going, and I liked the idea of a farewell concert. I rounded up the guys for our last gig, packed my Chevy truck with our equipment, and we headed down to Birmingham.

After we finished performing, I was curious to meet Manfredi, the mysterious man who organized this national meet-up. I asked when we'd get to talk to him, wondering if he'd have any interest in a bulk purchase for his crew of some of the CDs I'd been importing. I was promptly informed by a skinny, red-haired boy who lived on the property that "that scumbag" Manfredi wouldn't be attending because he had been arrested on illegal weapons charges the night before and was being held for further questioning in several cases allegedly involving sexual indecency and forced sexual misconduct with a minor.

"Excuse me. What the fuck did you just say?"

"Yup," said the freckled teenager, "Will's been molesting most of us who live here with him, and we finally turned him in."

It turned out several underage boys—many of them disillusioned runaways—had been living with Manfredi on the compound, and he gave them food, water, shelter, and an "education" in exchange for sex. The story I was told was that after he rescued these boys from a life on the streets and indoctrinated them over time to worship him, turning them into burgeoning neo-Nazis, he'd sexually abuse them and then threaten to expose them as homosexuals if they said a word.

Had Manfredi been there when I found out, he would not have made it off his own mountain alive.

By now Lisa had begun pressuring me heavily about my lingering involvement with the movement. She'd always been afraid for me, but now she was also feeling underappreciated. My involvement was taking time away from her and from our son.

She was right. Despite my efforts to keep my life with Lisa apart from my racist activities, the two worlds were rubbing against each other. The first incident happened not long into the marriage.

Again I'd been arrested. I was driving some Hammerskins visiting from Milwaukee to get some late-night food when they started a ruckus in the restaurant with a few inebriated jocks. As the stealthy undercover cops who'd been tailing us from my house to the restaurant showed up with flashing lights and guns drawn, all the visiting skinheads fled and left me holding the bag.

The prosecutor couldn't prove I'd physically assaulted anyone—I hadn't—so I was only found guilty of mob action and disorderly conduct, not assault and battery. I was placed on house arrest for thirty days. Had the Pakistani restaurant owner not stepped forward on his own and testified on my behalf that I wasn't party to the fight, it would have meant certain jail time for me. Again, my prejudices collided with reason.

At the police station, the cops pressured me for two hours to give up the names of the others involved, in return for dropping the charges against me. I had no interest in cooperating with them. I was pissed at the Milwaukee guys for coming into my town and starting trouble that I was left to clean up, but I was no rat.

A second incident that understandably freaked Lisa out happened when Devin was five months old. I'd been tipped off by one of our double agents that a rival Anti gang was planning to detonate a pipe bomb at our home on the anniversary of their founding. I rushed home from work, sent Lisa and Devin to her mother's house where they'd be safe, and rounded up six of my most loyal associates. We stood watch all night with loaded rifles and shotguns pointed out of the windows, ready for someone to approach in the darkness.

Around midnight, we saw a figure appear from the shadows. Instantly, we turned our guns on him. My finger lay poised on the hair trigger of my AK-47, waiting for a reason to squeeze it.

"Don't shoot!" one of the gunmen yelled. "It's Steve!" Steve was a young probationary Hammerskin, arriving late for the vigil.

I secured my weapon and set it down, leaned my back against the wall. For the third time in my life, I'd almost shot someone. Each time, it was someone innocent. I shook to think how close we'd come to opening fire on a friend. This only increased my anger that someone was threatening my family.

How dare they put me in this situation?

Fuming, I ordered everyone back to their positions. We resumed our patrol. Hours passed, but nothing ever happened.

By morning we were exhausted from lack of sleep, aggravated from the pointless watch, and Lisa was furious at me for worrying her and her mother for no good reason.

I wasn't able to pinpoint when it had begun to turn, but married life had become a lot more tense. I adored Devin and still treasured my marriage, but Lisa and I had begun arguing all the time about my extracurricular activities. I looked for reasons to go away because the fights wore me down.

One such weekend in the winter of 1993 I retreated to a concert in Buffalo, New York, to blow off some steam after another one of our nastier arguments. Skinhead bands had descended on Buffalo from New Jersey and Atlantic City. Music and beer propelled the crowd and, before we knew it, some skinheads took advantage of the copious amounts of liquid courage they'd ingested, and a ragtag army of drunken would-be warriors took to the tenement building across the street from the club. They busted down doors and beat and dragged some innocent black and Latino families forcefully out of bed in the middle of the night. Police sirens echoed through the darkness. I just got in my truck and drove back home to Chicago.

Despite my growing reservations about the whole white-power movement, I found it very hard to let go. It had been my entire identity from the age of fourteen, and I still savored my role as a leader.

By August of 1993, word arrived that Big Ed from Bound For Glory had pegged me to replace him as the director of the Northern Hammerskins division. It meant I'd oversee the Hammerskin Nation operations for all of the states north of the Mason-Dixon line. Nearly three hundred skinheads would be under my direct command.

Big Ed had been leading the group for four years already, but he wanted to focus more on his band, since they'd been touring and recording almost nonstop since our concert together in Germany.

Part of me was thrilled that I'd been handpicked to lead a part of what was becoming known across the U.S. as the most feared and violent white supremacist group, but more undeniable was my inner voice nagging me with questions about what I was involved in, telling me to step away from it all.

The next month, while I was at Big Ed's home in St. Paul, Minnesota, ironing out the details of the transition, we received a call from the Blood & Honour skinhead crew in England with unimaginable news. Skrewdriver's lead singer and driving force, Ian Stuart, had been killed in a car crash earlier that morning. We were stunned. Ian Stuart was a folk hero to many skinheads, including an inspirational role model for me. The death made me think about Clark Martell, the other onetime role model I'd lost, the man who'd been responsible for introducing me to the boisterous music of Skrewdriver and the skinhead lifestyle when I was a boy, all of thirteen and a half years old. Where might he be? The last bit of correspondence from him that I remembered opening came with a Polaroid picture of his new prison tattoo—on the center of his forehead was a freshly inked German eagle holding a swastika. Clark looked haggard, sick. On the back of the photo was a simple, hand-drawn smiley face with the barely legible words, "See ya when I see ya! Long live the Aryan Goddess! 14/88. CM."

While I sat and mourned the passing of Ian Stuart, I wondered where the man who had once promised to save my life would find his own safety. Word spread that shortly after his release from prison, Clark had fled the halfway house and made his way into Michigan, where he'd gotten into an argument at the Detroit clubhouse and stabbed a Hammerskin with a screwdriver. I may have been stubborn and hard to reach under the clouds of my misguided ideology, but the irony of that rumor wasn't lost on me.

REVOLUTION
STARTS
HERE!

22

ORGANIZED CHAOS

Collecting an unemployment check and selling a few compact discs may have taken some of the sting out of being laid off from my road construction job every winter, but Lisa and I were still barely scraping by. Furthermore, the wonderment and magic of being newlyweds and having a baby as part of our family had been eroded by the harsh reality of our constant fighting, and we sometimes were hardly speaking. Our mobile home honeymoon was over.

When she got angry, Lisa would let me know she wished she'd gone to college instead of marrying me.

"I'm home all day long doing laundry and cleaning the house, and I never leave to do anything but buy baby food and diapers," she told me. "Why don't you pitch in and help instead of going to your stupid meetings and running around with your useless friends?"

"You mean the friends I hardly get to spend time with anymore because I'm working seventy-hour weeks?" I would counter.

Inevitably she'd cry. And then the baby would cry. "God, I wish I'd gone to school so I could go out and get a real job," she would confess. "So I wouldn't have to depend on you to raise my child."

"He's *our* child, Lisa, and I support you both so you don't have to work. So you can sit at home on your ass all day." Even at the time I knew it was a bald-faced lie. One I instantly wished I could take back.

Our fights would continue with Lisa reminding me that I was an absent father and husband, that I didn't know what it's like to raise a child, that everything was handed to me for my whole life and I didn't even appreciate it. She pointed out that even though I resented my mother and father for not being there, I ignored my own child more than they ever could have done to me. "Devin doesn't even know who you are and, frankly, I don't want him to!"

That was usually my cue to grab the car keys and slam the door on my way out. Her words pierced me so deeply that I was afraid of not being able to control my temper. The truth often hurts more than any lie can. I'd find one of my skinhead pals to drink and commiserate with, and a few hours later I'd return. Lisa would be locked in the bedroom with Devin, and I'd sleep it off on the couch until it was time for work the next morning.

Lisa felt trapped and said she never slept while I was away attending to movement affairs. She became resolute in her objections to anything at all I did with skinheads. Not only did she despise the racism and senseless violence, but she worried constantly that I was going to end up in jail or dead, leaving her to fend for our child herself.

In our calmer moments, we talked about how we were growing apart. We both felt overburdened with responsibilities. We both continued to imply that the other one had it easier. And after expending every possible option, our ultimate solution to save our marriage was to do yet another foolish thing—we selfishly rationalized that if we had another child, we'd somehow create an opportunity to bind ourselves closer to each other and thus repair our fractured relationship. So we began to try for another baby. Giving ourselves this new purpose did somehow rekindle our affection for each other, and when Devin was a little over a year old, Lisa was expecting again.

Big Ed called late one night, shortly after we received the news that Lisa was pregnant, to congratulate me and set a date to meet again. With his busy traveling schedule and the sudden news of Ian Stuart's passing, we hadn't gotten around to finalizing the leadership transfer of the Northern Hammerskins.

"The last thing we need to do to make this official," he said, "is get you on the phone with Shane Becker." Becker was national director for the Hammerskin Nation and one of the Dallas Hammerskin founders who'd been at the Naperville meeting in 1988. "It'll be tricky since he's still in federal prison, but if we set a date and a specific time window for you to be by your phone, we can make it work."

"Ed, I've actually been meaning to call you about that." I hemmed and hawed before actually getting to the point. I could sense him shifting in his chair on the other end of the line. Finally, I could avoid it no longer. "With work and the new baby and all," I said, "I'm going to have to bow out of the running."

"Well, that's disappointing." I could tell by his voice, without him saying the actual words, that he understood my dilemma. We were close friends, and I'd confided in him multiple times about my marital woes. "I understand. Take care of that family of yours, and come see us again soon in St. Paul. Julie and our girls would love some company."

"Will do, Ed."

The next day, while I was packing a lunch before heading to work, I received a call from a Texas correctional institution. It was Shane Becker asking if I'd reconsider my decision to step away. After a few pleasantries, I politely declined the offer and wished him well.

Though I had, faced with the dilemma of going all in with the Hammerskins or preserving my marriage, chosen my marriage, I still selfishly planned to continue to participate in the white-power movement.

I hadn't stopped importing white-power CDs from Europe to supplement my income. Selling so many of them on the side, the idea to open a record store and to be my own boss took root. Not only could my shop carry music, but I could sell posters, T-shirts, boots, braces, and other accessories I knew skins and punks would buy. I could use my entrepreneurial knack to both feed my family and keep the local skinhead scene going strong, without having to leave either behind.

My leadership and steadfast involvement over the last six years had helped grow the American white-power skinhead movement from its earliest roots—the legacy bestowed upon me by the founding triumvirate of Clark Martell, Carmine Paterno, and Chase Sargent—but between the responsibilities of working and taking care of a family and Lisa's constant fears for my safety, I found little time anymore for rallies, recruiting new members, organizing the crew, performing with my band, and the things that had catapulted me into a leadership position in the first place.

With a store selling our unique brand of music and feeding our culture, I could contribute to the cause in a less prominent, but still significant, way. The music I'd sell would keep us straight on our priorities; it would inspire newcomers to join our mission; and the flexibility of being my own boss would allow me to spend more time with my family.

Lisa didn't object to me opening a store. She wasn't so sure it would work, but she agreed we needed the money and it was worth the risk. Perhaps she was just happy to see me interested in something beyond white-power rallies, even if it involved the music we would often play at them. Hungry for professional fulfillment in my life, desperate to earn a better living, wanting an opportunity to prove my capabilities as a husband and father, I gambled our paltry savings and a three-thousand-dollar loan from Lisa's mother to ramp up my idea quickly. I headed out to find the perfect spot for Chaos Records—the name I'd settled on months earlier. I surged with pride at the thought that this would support my expanding family while still allowing me to remain connected to the movement.

I signed a cheap lease for a vacant storefront near a busy intersection just west of Blue Island's border. The space had been sitting empty for a while, a fact I used to negotiate a favorable deal on the rent. I built out the inside of the store myself—installing a counter, racks, shelving—and paid an artist friend from high school fifty bucks to airbrush the walls with apocalyptic images better suiting the giant "anarchy" symbol that served as the "A" in the red neon Chaos Records sign glowing in the window. I hung dozens of busted vinyl records from the ceiling with fishing line, plastered my old punk rock posters all over the walls, and tiled the floor in a black-and-white checkerboard ska pattern. I spent weeks carefully choosing and ordering my music inventory—all independent or underground music you couldn't find anyplace else in the area, at least not at mainstream record shops like Record Town or Sam Goody.

While selling white-power music was my bread and butter, I also carried more run-of-the-mill Oi!, punk rock, ska, hardcore, rockabilly, black metal, and hip-hop music. This was a legitimate business, after all, and I needed a diverse inventory that would bring paying customers through the doors and cool any potential heat some of my inventory might bring. But it was the white-power music and my regular movement customers that were my mainstay and kept me in business.

Cops were on to the store the moment it opened. Squad cars routinely lurked in the parking lot, the police expecting trouble. I was selling subversive music that few, if any, other shops in the country sold. They were no doubt concerned my store would be a front for bad stuff. Perhaps it was one of Chaos Records' two taglines that I used in print advertisements and spray painted on the walls inside the store that roused their ire: "The Revolution Starts Here" and "Fuck Peace. I Want Chaos!"

I'm not sure if they realized that while I was still looked upon by the movement as the primary Illinois figurehead among white-power skinheads, I was now removed from all the daily activities, the responsibilities for which I had transferred to veterans in my crew. I no longer wrote letters or sent out pamphlets, hadn't been to an out-of-state gathering in almost a year, and I'd stopped recruiting altogether. While there were others within my crew still pounding the pavement, our diminished numbers were evident.

Not long after I opened the record store, a couple of undercover cops wandered in, two guys in their early thirties wearing street clothes, apathetic and clean-cut as soldiers in boot camp.

Smirking, I walked over to them, held my hand out, and said in my politest tone, "Nice to meet you, officers. Let me guess, you're either here to pick up the new Cradle of Filth album or to buy tickets for the Anal Cunt in-store acoustic show we're having next week. Either way, I can help you. Cash or credit?"

Red-faced, they looked at each other, shrugged, and after pretending to browse for a minute to save face, left.

Before I opened my shop, I would have given them hell, told them they had no right to trespass on my property, and kicked them out for being traitors to their race. But I chose not to do business that way. My kids' livelihood depended on the community supporting the store—or at least not despising it enough to rally to put it out of business.

And because I had to learn to depend on my community in this way, I unwittingly became more tolerant of those people whose views didn't line up with mine—until the day Sammy, the black anti-racist skinhead, entered my shop.

I kept a loaded 9mm handgun behind the counter, just in case. When Black Sammy and three of his fresh-cut minions walked in, it didn't take long for the pistol to find its place tucked within reach behind my belt.

I'd been paging through catalogs of upcoming new releases, marking off titles I wanted to stock the following month when Sammy and his crew strolled in. My blood froze when I casually glanced up and saw him standing there in the doorway, his blue bomber jacket hanging off his skinny black frame, dark eyes brooding, his henchmen unflinching behind him. We held each other's stares for a territorially awkward fifteen seconds. "You got any Skrewdriver poppin' up in this joint?" Sammy quipped as he made his way through the front door of the record store. "How about some White American Youth or Final Solution?"

Black Sammy was a well-known old-school skin who had co-founded the anti-racist group Skinheads of Chicago with Dwight, another tough black skinhead who'd grown up in Chicago's housing projects. They found each other as lonely, young punk rockers going to shows on the North Side of the city, "urban" anomalies among an ocean of angsty white suburbanites. After CASH members began passing out Romantic Violence flyers in front of punk shows at clubs like Cabaret Metro and Medusa's in 1985, the two decided they would counter Clark and his crew's advances by forming a rival anti-racist skinhead gang.

"I think you might be in the wrong place, Sammy," I replied, staring him down as I stepped from behind the counter. I was alone in the store. My hand was hovering behind my back, near my piece.

"Come on, Picciolini. I know you guys keep that Nazi shit behind the counter." He sounded serious, notwithstanding the swastika inked on the center of his forehead. Sammy never addressed that, and it had never made sense to any of us white-power skins.

"Sammy, you and your guys are welcome here." The words came out of my mouth before I realized I'd said them. "But I don't want any trouble."

"Good, now give me all your motherfucking Skrewdriver." He approached as my hand nervously adjusted my waistband.

"All right, I'll bite," I said, snapping into action. "Which album do you want?" I moved my way back over to the counter, creating a barrier between me and the four goons who were now littered about the shop.

"All of them. I want everything you've got." Fuck. Here we go, I thought. I fingered the trigger, nervous over where this could go. As I knelt behind the counter to grab the box of CDs, scenarios flashed through my head. How could I take care of Sammy and still have time to track and take down the other three Antis if they came at me with weapons of their own. Surely it would be justified self-defense in response to a robbery. I neglected to reflect on the fact that the gun I'd be committing this quadruple homicide with was registered to a Mexican factory worker whose identity I'd stolen.

"How much are they?"

My itchy finger disengaged the safety as I slowly rose up with the gun hidden beneath the box of CDs.

"Do you take credit cards?" Sammy asked.

"What?" I wasn't sure if I'd registered what he said.

"Do you take credit cards? I ain't speaking Swahili, motherfucker." His guys laughed.

I carefully returned the readied gun behind my back to my waistband. "Yeah. MasterCard and Visa. No American Express." I turned to scan the barcodes into the computer. Hesitantly, I turned to him. "Sammy, why the fuck are you buying Skrewdriver?"

"Why the fuck do you sell it?" He paused. "That shit is dope, nigga!"

We spent the next thirty minutes discussing other "dope" skinhead bands and reminiscing about the early days of the Chicago skinhead scene. I laughed when he told me that he hated Bound For Glory because their music was "too goddamn metal," but WAY was "a'ight for some white-boy music." I thanked him and told him I'd pass along the feedback to Big Ed.

Before they left, Sammy and his pals spent more than three hundred dollars buying music and T-shirts that afternoon. It was by far the biggest receipt I'd gotten from a single sale since I first opened the store. Before I knew it, we were shaking hands, and a bizarre smile was forming on my face. What could I say? The ideological delusions that had led me so far astray were crumbling right before my eyes. I was shocked when I considered how an hour ago I would have simply dismissed him as less than me. He was just another lost soul trying to grope his way through the confusion of this mixed-up world, and frankly it appeared he was doing a much better job of it than I was.

Once they were gone, I unloaded my gun and locked it in the safe in the back room. I'd come too close to murder again that day. I would make sure that it was the last time.

Over time, dozens more Antis came in to buy the more apolitical Oi! and ska music they would otherwise have had to trek twenty miles into the city to get. I had been their sworn enemy for most of the last seven years, but I offered good prices and a vast selection to choose from. I even carried titles that record shops in the city wouldn't stock, some of the anti-racist skinhead bands.

Regardless, I couldn't put a gun in their face or chase them out of my store or not sell to them if I wanted my business to provide for my family. So more and more I chatted with them, made small talk, tried to remember their names and answer their questions. I was surprised to discover how decent they were. Even more, they were *people*, people with whom I had much more common with than the ones I had surrounded myself with since I was fourteen. I was beginning to notice the little experiences that bind us humans together.

Meanwhile, my white-power customers dwindled. I started hearing less and less from Kubiak and the crew. I chalked it up to the fact that they were usually broke, or that none of them were married or had kids to support, and they probably thought hanging around at a record store all day wasn't as exciting as being out on the street raining terror. I'd spent so many years immersing myself in the movement that the diversity of my customer base continued to fascinate me. I began to meet gay and Jewish customers. Our conversations were brief, guarded at first, but slowly we got to know each other through our shared interest in music. And they kept coming back. I was indebted to their business, and I found myself thinking clearly, "These are good people. I don't want to hurt them." We swapped stories about old concerts we'd been to. I met punk rock customers of every color—metal heads from Latin America, a rockabilly band from Algeria, a gay Christian couple shopping for underground death metal lounge music. (I didn't have it, but I ordered it for them.) And I met my first transgender, half-Asian, half-Puerto Rican atheist Jew. I'd started opening up to people who looked different from me, and life had become interesting in a way I never would have guessed it could.

It felt good to get a little glimpse of the way my life had been before I was radicalized, back when I had friends who didn't care what my "beliefs" were. I suddenly became aware that the bitterness that had surrounded me had begun to atrophy, and empathy had trickled in, filling the void.

In August of 1994, shortly before our second child was due, I decided to attend a concert that was being held in memory of Ian Stuart in Racine, Wisconsin. Resistance Records, an upstart American white-power label whose music I'd sold tons of through the store, was hosting the highly anticipated event.

Lisa was far from happy I'd decided to go, but she knew I'd kept my promise to step back from movement activities to spend more time with the family. She recognized this concert was a one-time thing and especially significant to me. Stuart had been one of my musical inspirations, someone I'd corresponded with and emulated over the years. What worried her was that the concert would be well attended. And where groups of skinheads gathered, trouble was certain to follow.

I minimized the likelihood of that, reassuring Lisa I wouldn't do anything to jeopardize our mending relationship and that I'd drive the two hours back home as soon as the concert ended. I pointed out that I didn't consider myself a racial activist anymore. I'd even decided to stop selling white-power music in the store. In light of my new friendships, even the racist terms I'd bandied about had fallen out of my vocabulary. Not because I wanted to sell more music, but because I'd come to respect them, and I didn't want to insult anyone.

Reassured somewhat, Lisa hugged me and told me to come home safe.

When I arrived, the concert hall was humming with energy. The audience was also crawling with old friends. Embraces and shared stories filled the night.

"Well, look who it is. How's it going, stranger?" It was Big Ed.

"Hey, man. Good to see you," I replied as we shared a bear hug.

"How's that record store of yours doing? Are you carrying the new Bound For Glory record?"

"Actually, I've been thinking of scaling back a bit on the white-power music. It hasn't been selling like it used to. Rock-O-Rama raised their prices on me, so I have to charge more and I guess people just can't afford it." I was lying through my teeth.

"Really? That's too bad." He seemed to want to say more than he had. "Well, maybe you can bring in some of that jigaboo rap music to boost your sales." He laughed. I felt uneasy. By now the first band had taken the stage and was ripping into their first song.

"Well, hey, man, it was good to see you. Pretty cool that No Remorse was able to make it all the way from England to play, even if it is under somber circumstances."

"Yeah. I've gotta get ready for our set." He gave me a parting embrace and started to walk away. "Oh, that reminds me, some guy claiming to be from your crew sent me a letter a few weeks back. I think you should read it."

"Really?" I was genuinely surprised. "What did it say?"

"He was saying all kinds of nonsensical shit about you. Julie's got my bag. I'll give you the letter after the show, and you can take it home and stick it up his ass. You should definitely read it." I said I would. "It ain't good," he added.

I was worried. Who the hell was the letter from? Nobody had said anything to me back home. I hadn't been hanging out, but nobody seemed too upset by it. I knew a few of the guys weren't too happy about some of the new music I was selling, but they'd been in the shop since I'd started carrying it and never mentioned anything about it other than ribbing me a bit.

I couldn't get my conversation with Big Ed out of my mind. I ran through every possible scenario I could think of. Had I slighted someone? Said something to offend one of them? Just then No Remorse took the stage, and the nagging voices in my head dissipated.

Before blasting into song, their singer, whom I'd shared some correspondence with and become friendly with over the years and whose music I had grown up on and learned from as a young skinhead, began his set with a moving speech about Ian Stuart. And for a moment, I let myself be pulled back in, high on the ephemera and intensity of the night. The music pounded in my veins as a thousand skinheads flowed like rapids around me. But the high was short-lived.

Less than an hour after the concert ended, tragedy struck. While buying beer in a nearby convenience store, Joe Rowan, a fellow Hammerskin and the lead singer of the band Nordic Thunder, was shot and killed in a skirmish with black youths. Joe was a friend, someone I'd known for several years and had grown to respect. We'd spoken at the venue less than twenty minutes before. Joe was so proud of his children and carried on affectionately about them and showed me their photographs, which he kept in his wallet. Now he had left his two young babies fatherless and a young, single mother unequipped to care for them.

After that, I didn't care enough to wait around for Big Ed to give me the letter.

I could no longer deny my growing disgust with this miserable existence I'd created. This life wasn't for me anymore. I could see this fractured perpetual motion machine of unending violence and despair for what it was.

23

WHITE REVOLUTION

THE EXPERIENCE OF SEEING clearly after peering through a lens of distorted ideology for so long was indescribable. All these details about the strangers I passed every day—the way they held their hands, the character lines on their faces, the gestures that connect us but also make us unique—seemed visible for the first time. I still sometimes sensed myself judging people, my mind jumping to the prejudices I taught it, but when I challenged myself I learned that I simply couldn't justify or reconcile those prejudices any longer.

Memories of the past seven years flashed through my mind, and they made me angry. I thought about the Ku Klux Klan with their ridiculous dunce caps and tablecloth clown costumes; the racist sovereign constitutionalists who carried automatic weapons to church and felt that man-made laws didn't apply to them; the Christian Identity believers that distorted the Bible to suit their perverse dogmatism that turned God into a vengeful Aryan warlord who sought to slay the mud races, which they say are creations of the Devil; the revisionist historians who claimed the Holocaust never happened and six million Jews somehow magically evaporated from the earth; the laughable American Nazi Party storm troopers dressed as if every day were a Third Reich Halloween, with their brown Boy Scout shirts and fancy culottes; the racial Odinists who believed that fairy Viking gods who lived in the clouds would strike down the dark-skinned infidels with bolts of lightning and a crack of Thor's hammer; and the neo-Nazi skinhead gangbanger thugs who fooled themselves into believing that they had an ounce of courage or pride running through their veins, when in reality they were filled with a volatile cocktail of cheap beer and self-hatred. Now, when I looked into the mirror I saw a hollow shell of a man—a stranger—assembled from those same toxic elements staring back at me.

For one-third of my life I'd chewed and swallowed gristly bits of each one of those twisted ideologies, and now all I felt like doing was jamming my fingers down my throat and vomiting them all up into the nearest toilet. I felt like a dope fiend, except I was detoxing from selfish power and control, always craving more and living on a razor's edge, perpetually looking to score the next hateful fix.

For years all I could think about was how I got so horribly off track. I'd blamed everyone but myself for what I believed had been taken away from me as a young boy. I was angry with my parents for abandoning me for their careers, and I took my misplaced aggression out on the world, blaming those whom I failed to make an effort to understand, rather than taking responsibility for my own feelings and actions.

And because I was too afraid of my true emotions, I ended up blaming others—blacks, gays, Jews, and anyone else who I thought wasn't like me—for problems in my own life they couldn't possibly have contributed to. My unfounded panic quickly, and unjustly, manifested itself as venomous hatred.

Now, people I had once terrorized were willing to knowingly put aside the evil I'd stood for, become my paying customers, and go out of their way to connect with me. I knew I didn't deserve their kindness. They were aware of my entire sordid history, yet they never condemned me or kicked out my taillights or spray-painted obscenities on my store. We had to *rely* on one another, they taught me, not *hurt* one another.

This truth was at first excruciatingly painful and shameful, but it was the key that unlocked the fortress in which I'd imprisoned my soul.

Everyone from my old crew had stopped visiting the shop. They grew certain that the jumble of outsiders who'd made their way into my circle were pushing them out. They'd grown weary of my excuses for why I couldn't come out and spend time with them. Before long, I began to hear whispers that I'd lost my edge, that I was a capitalist looking to profit from the movement. I became nervous, afraid to come clean about my feelings. So I did the cowardly thing: I squashed the rumors as quickly as I heard them by making an example of those who spoke them, shaming them. Discrediting them. Turning the tables. Even Kubiak and I had grown distant.

"What the hell is that race traitor doing here?" I heard the new young face quip as I stepped over a young fresh-cut who was laid out drunk on the steps leading down into Kubiak's wood-paneled basement. I'd decided to stop by on my way home from work to drop off a surplus of literature I had been storing at the shop. "Shouldn't he be at his record store, sticking his nose up some kike's ass?" A small group assembled around him silently chuckled behind the beer cans pressed to their lips.

"What the fuck did you say?"

I hadn't ever noticed this kid before tonight, but the deadness in his eyes reminded me of something I'd seen in my own a thousand times.

"I said you're a nigger-loving faggot who sucks circumcised Jew dick."

Operating on pure muscle memory, I pushed off the bottom stair and lunged at him. The crowd scrambled to separate us, and Kubiak reached in from behind and put me in a chokehold.

"You have to fucking go," Kubiak grunted as he struggled to drag me away. "You can't be here."

I'd become a pariah, and as scared as I was of what the consequences might be for my perceived betrayal, it was also the first time in my life that I was satisfied with the feeling of *not* belonging.

I soon found myself preferring the solitude of the store to anyplace else and spent at least twelve hours a day there, which did not sit well with my wife.

Neither the coming of our second child, nor the extra money the store was bringing in, was making much of a difference in our marriage. I began avoiding Lisa again, tired of the renewed fighting, weary of the accusations about not spending enough time with her and Devin. Though Lisa was happy that I'd begun to leave the movement behind, she couldn't ignore the fact that I was treating my own wife and son like I'd complained my parents had treated me.

Our second son, Brandon, was born on November 18, 1994, just after my twenty-first birthday and almost two years to the day after our son Devin. His birth was every bit as moving and magical as his brother's had been, and Lisa and I instantly fell madly in love with him.

But his birth could not save our marriage. If anything could have, it would have been our children.

It was too late.

I knew we were doomed the night I came home late again to Lisa strapping Devin and Brandon into their car seats. I'd missed dinner, just as I had the night before. One look at her swollen eyes that avoided mine like poison, and I could tell she had been crying. She said she wasn't in love with me anymore. She stared at me, holding Devin's tiny hand and clasping four-month-old Brandon to her chest. Those words hurt me more than any argument we'd ever had, and I knew at that moment all hope for our marriage was lost. Lisa brought our boys out to the car, and over her shoulder she yelled that she wanted a divorce. She left for her grandparents' tiny trailer on the lake in Michigan—the very same one where we'd spent our first night as joyful newlyweds—with our children in tow. I stood in the street and watched my family vanish into the darkness before me. I'd set out to give them everything, but instead I had selfishly hijacked their lives. I knew I had no right to stop them from leaving.

I spent the next two solemn hours packing a canvas duffel bag with the only belongings I felt entitled to—a couple T-shirts, two pairs of worn-out Levis, an armful of underwear and socks, and the heavy Doc Martens on my feet. I slept on the floor in the back room of my shop, next to a stack of broken records.

At daybreak the following morning, I knocked on my parents' door and asked to move back into the basement apartment below them that I'd made my home when I was fifteen.

Just like that.

Back to my Nazi skinhead frat-boy dorm room, dusty and stale, which served as a constant reminder of my failure. Not even Buddy, now eleven years old, wanted to hang out with me.

"Hey, Buddy. I could use some help doing inventory at the record store. Want to come to work with me tomorrow?"

"I'm going to the movies with Flaco. Maybe some other time."

I'd abandoned him for the movement, and now it was his turn to abandon me. Leaning against the counter, tired and alone after work that night, I realized that I'd been exactly like my parents. I'd made with my family all the mistakes I blamed my parents for making and then some. I'd made myself too busy earning a living to make time for my family. And I could no longer pretend that it was some working-class desire to put food on the table that had kept me away from them. It was my egotistical drive to be respected. To be a hero. When all I needed to do to be those things was just pay attention to what was right in front of me the entire time.

When all was said and done, the only thing I'd accomplished over the course of my long evenings at the store was to become someone I didn't respect. Not only did Chaos Records fail to fulfill my desire to provide for my family, but even worse, it broke us. After I pulled all the racist music from the inventory, which had accounted for the bulk of the store's sales, my revenue plummeted, and before long I couldn't afford to keep the doors open. Two short months after Lisa and I split up I liquidated and shuttered the store.

We both decided Lisa should keep the house, and in our divorce proceedings the judge awarded her primary custody of our boys. I was destitute, with no job, no home, no friends, and I no longer lived with my sons—the two most essential beings remaining in my life.

Four months later, on the morning of April 19, 1995—one day before neo-Nazis across the globe would be celebrating Adolf Hitler's 106th birthday—white supremacist Timothy McVeigh drove toward the Alfred P. Murrah Federal Building in Oklahoma City, Oklahoma, carrying a 4,800-pound fertilizer bomb in the back of his rented Ryder truck, where he detonated it, killing 168 innocent people—including nineteen children—and injuring many hundreds more. McVeigh had with him an envelope containing pages from *The Turner Diaries*—the fictional account of Earl Turner and an army of white revolutionaries who ignite a race war by blowing up FBI headquarters using a truck bomb.

It was the same book that Clark Martell had given me when I was fourteen, and that I'd read over and over, the very same book that I had kept stuffed in my coat pocket for almost seven years.

24

WALK ALONE

FOR THE NEXT FIVE YEARS I withdrew from the world and sank into an ever-deepening depression that saw me wanting to sleep in just a little while longer each morning until, eventually, I would run completely out of daylight. I'd open my eyes, hoping the darkness surrounding me meant that I was dead. I didn't know who I was, what my place in the world should be, or if I even cared enough about myself to attempt to remedy my miserable situation.

I'd lost everything that held any real value in my life. My wife and children were no longer part of my daily routine. I'd long since alienated myself from my parents, grandparents, and brother. My social framework and business had both collapsed. I found it painful to muster the energy to seek meaningful employment, and when I did force myself to find work—which I was only ever able to do because I desperately wanted to support my children—the best I could do was to toil away in a part-time, minimum-wage job. I felt as alone as my former fourteen-year-old self in that dead-end alley nearly thirteen years before. In the end, the only way I knew how to destroy the convoluted world I had created for myself was to suffer under the weight of it.

Christian Picciolini (Photo by Meredith Goldberg)

I needed sustenance—both physical and spiritual—and something had to get me out of the basement apartment in which I spent my days feeling sorry for myself, so when an acquaintance told me about a temp job with the computer firm IBM, I saw no other choice but to leap at it. Never mind I didn't know a damn thing about technology or hardware or software. I had confidence in my ability to fake it until I made it. I needed to stand on my own two feet, and I had two young kids who still depended on me to be their father.

I'd blown it with them so far, but I was determined to make up for it and to be sure they never lacked for anything. When I could see out of my depressed state, I resolved again to be the parent to them I'd always wanted mine to be for me, to spend more time with them—as much time as I possibly could, every weekend. I'd find out what interested them and do everything I could to encourage their dreams. If they played sports, I'd never miss a game. I'd make time to coach them. If they liked science, I'd buy them chemistry sets and microscopes and telescopes, and we'd visit the best museums so they could see what amazing things are possible if only they have the courage to dream them.

I ended up landing the job with IBM. My first assignment was working as the project manager's assistant on a large-scale computer installation job at Illinois School District 218, the same school district that included Eisenhower and PIE, where I'd gone so many years before. And who should I run into on my first week on the job but Mr. Johnny Holmes, the African American security guard at whom I had spewed all my racist bitterness on the day I was escorted out in handcuffs.

"Damn," I said when I saw him, ducking around a corner. "What the hell . . ."

My new colleague gave me a curious look. "What? You know the chief of police?"

I almost swallowed my tongue. "Chief of police? He's the security guard."

"Hardly. He's the top cop now and is on the school board." My co-worker looked me over. "So, you in trouble with him or what?"

"I made his life hell when I was a so-called student here," I said. "We almost came to blows once. I was an ignorant... racist... asshole and caused all kinds of problems for him."

"Racist?" she straightened up and asked, surprised. "You?"

Her disbelief washed over me like a cleansing rain. For years during my involvement in the white-power movement, nothing made me prouder than my racist reputation, and now here was someone who was incredulous to hear that word associated with me. It had been five years since I'd left it all behind, though I had still not publicly confronted my past. Ashamed and scared, I had run from it, struggling to stay ahead of its grasp and afraid of being judged in the same ways I judged others.

I had been living in fear for the last five years, hoping that my past wouldn't catch up with me and prevent me from moving forward professionally and socially, and terrified that the hundreds, maybe even thousands, of violent people that I helped create might someday seek me out and hurt me or my children. During my time in the movement, it was encouraged to vilify anyone who left the movement as a "race traitor." It was considered an open invitation for a brutal assault or murder. My colleague's kindness toward me helped me realize the right way to handle the situation I was in. I tore after my former nemesis and spotted him as he was leaving the building. I could feel my hands shaking with nervousness, but for the first time, I ran toward something in these school halls instead of away from it. "Mr. Holmes!" I cried. "Hold on, please."

He turned, his smile abruptly fading as he recognized me.

"Excuse me. Do you remember me, Mr. Holmes?"

"You're hard to forget," he said, his voice holding back any emotion.

"I want to tell you... tell you I'm sorry," I said, catching my breath.

"All those terrible things I said. What I did. My hatred. I made your life miserable when I attended school here. I'd take it back if I could, though I understand that I can't—those memories are stuck with each of us and I just want to apologize. Thank you for helping to show me what it means to live a life of dignity even when I didn't deserve it."

He studied me intently. After a short time, he held out his hand and gave a slight nod. "I'm glad to hear it, Mr. Picciolini. True freedom from our demons requires great amounts of sacrifice and pain. I believe you know what I'm talking about. It's your responsibility now to tell the world what healed you. Welcome home."

Tears stung my eyes as our hands connected, and I looked down to see hands that were once squeezed into fists longing to lash out now locked together in forgiveness.

The concept was pure. The only hope I had of trying to wash away the evil I'd paid tribute to was by exposing it to the light.

At eighteen, I'd stood on stage in a cathedral in Germany, cries of "Heil Hitler!" punctuating the roar of thousands of European skinheads shouting the name of my band.

At that very moment, I was responsible for the electricity in the air, the adrenaline coursing through throbbing veins, the sweat pouring down shaved heads.

I'd talked about how laws favoring blacks were taking white jobs, and how we were overburdened with unjust taxes used to support welfare programs, about the neighborhoods of law-abiding, hardworking white families being overrun with criminal minorities and their drugs.

The truth was my parents never lost jobs to any minorities. They struggled by the skin of their teeth to make good, like most Americans do, to support their families through hard work, to settle down somewhere safe and claim their slice of the American pie. When I chose to foolishly venture out onto that stage on a mission to demand respect rather than earn it, I didn't know then that I was running from something: I was running from my own fear of failure and self-hatred.

I was convinced being a brave warrior meant destroying the "enemy," battling anyone unlike me at any given moment, and spreading fear throughout the community. In truth, it's weakness that carries a bloody sword, and real strength comes from being willing to take arrows to the chest. To learn from your mistakes. To be vulnerable and honest and accept that sometimes you just don't know. To be human.

In the movement, our words to each other may have been about honor and pride, but I could now see looking back that when we spoke to the outside world, it was all deception, all bait-and-switch. Lies were our defense—our truth. To survive this Orwellian mind-set, we had to constantly close our eyes and master the art of perjury. The lie and the truth had to taste the same.

The French have a saying, *l'appel du vide*, "the call of the void." It describes that tiny voice in your head that even the most rational people might hear, that taunts you to jerk the steering wheel into oncoming traffic, or the feeling when you look over the edge of a steep precipice and become gripped with the fear of falling, but the terrifying impulse to throw yourself off the edge still beckons. In the five years since I had left the movement, I had heard that nagging little voice constantly, always whispering in my ear to find a way to try to kill what I'd helped create, but I was frightened of the consequences, and I didn't know how or where to start. It wasn't until I began to realize that the road to recovery started with me reopening my own wounds that I no longer wanted to silence that urge.

This stark realization was the beginning of a new life. Once I'd reached the point of finally letting go of my toxic shame completely, that's when change began to take hold. When I finally felt the pavement beneath me end and I reached the edge of that cliff, I had no interest in stopping to evaluate. I wasn't scared anymore. After years of not being honest with myself, I grew too tired to juggle the lies and hide the fears. I'd been committing suicide in daily increments. It was time to face the truth. I stepped hard on the gas and drove off that metaphorical cliff. I floored it, content that the demons inside of me were falling to their death. And only then, when I'd allowed that painful, symbolic death to occur—the twisted hunk of my former self burning on the sharp rocks below—only then could I rise from the rubble and begin anew.

My depression quickly began to fade, and the next few years seemed to fly by. IBM hired me on full-time, and I enjoyed a successful career in marketing and operations. While employed there, I jumped at an opportunity to take advantage of their educational assistance. In 2001, I enrolled at DePaul University, one of two colleges I'd originally been denied entrance to while still in alternative school, and I found myself a student once again. But this time, I welcomed it. I threw myself into my studies. While school had once been the bane of my existence, I now cherished every moment of it. I met students from all walks of life and bonded with them on levels I'd never let myself believe existed. Professors opened my mind with new ideas and theories. An endless world awakened. I embraced the diversity and graduated a double major in international business and international relations.

The high point of my college education came when I visited the United Nations in New York City as part of a global conference focused on the Millennium Development Goals. I learned about the horrific, all-too-common exploitation and trafficking of women and children, worldwide hunger, the AIDS pandemic, and the ravages of poverty and social-class discrimination. The whole experience made me realize how much work there was to be done all over the world to make life fair for people of all races, religious beliefs, genders, and sexual preferences.

Despite our tumultuous relationship, Lisa and I became good friends and committed co-parents. I finally realized how fortunate I was to have had her as a partner in raising our two boys.

With her help and my commitment, I honored my pledge to myself to be there for my kids. I seldom dated because I reserved my free time for them. I accompanied my boys to all their school functions and parent-teacher conferences, helped them with homework and science projects, and was there when they kicked their first soccer ball.

The only thing that filled me with as much joy as my time with my children was meeting Britton, the love of my life. Like me, she worked for IBM, but halfway across the country in a Dallas sales center. We communicated with each other about work regularly before meeting in person. It wasn't a case of love at first sight—it was love *before* first sight as we got to know each other through emails and phone calls. My main concern was that she would take one look at the old tattoos I'd been covering up with long sleeves, see the evidence of my past, and run. I knew hatred and prejudice were alien concepts to her, and I didn't believe she could ever love anyone with a history like mine.

But she is an amazing woman and saw beyond my mistakes to the man I had become. When we finally met in person after months of getting to know each other from afar, it was a Hollywood meeting. We ran into each other's arms and kissed before saying a single word. We will never stop kissing, stop loving, stop growing, and experiencing the wonders of life together.

Within eight months of that first embrace, Britton moved to Chicago, insisting on living in her own place so we could properly introduce her into the boys' lives over time and both be sure that it was the best situation for all of us. We married three years later, in 2005. I also reconciled with my parents. I know having me as their son was not easy. I tested them to their limits, and now that I am a parent myself, I understand why they made the choices they did. I was an obnoxiously arrogant, selfish, spoiled brat and never appreciated all the supportive and selfless sacrifices they made for me until I was faced with those same challenges myself. They loved me and did what they believed was right at the time to provide a better life for me and my brother, and I respect them for that.

After all I had done, all the pain and misery I caused, the hate I spread, the downright evil I perpetrated across the U.S. and even into Canada and Europe, I felt so incredibly fortunate to have a college education, an incredible wife, two terrific sons, a good relationship with my parents at last, and a life I could be proud of.

Then in one split second, everything changed.

25

SINS OF THE BROTHER

As BUDDY BECAME A TEENAGER, he grew distant, understanding that the "sometime" when I told him I'd spend time with him would never come. He was understandably resentful I'd left him behind, betrayed; soon he had begun misbehaving like I had, hanging out with street gangs. He earned himself a reputation like I had.

Like me, he drank. Unlike me during my skinhead days, he got into drugs. He spent time in jail for possession of marijuana and an illegal firearm. It was a small amount of weed, but the gun was enough to get him locked up. The judge sentenced him to do community service since it was his first offense, but Buddy wanted to prove he was tougher than me and demanded jail time instead. I worried about his choices, wrote to him and visited when he was locked up. I tried to reconnect, to find out what was going on with him and how I could help. I knew he still maintained friendships with people who were in gangs like the Latin Kings, and that worried me. He assured me he wasn't in a gang, but I worried that hanging out with those who were—whether he was officially a member or not—would lead to more trouble. When I moved back into my parents' basement after the divorce, I became more concerned about his choices. I tried talking to my parents, telling them where it would all lead. But they

Christian Picciolini and "Buddy," 1985

dismissed me, not having the courage to stand up to him, the same way they had feared me after I had humiliated and attacked them.

I had arguments with my brother about the path he was on, lecturing him even though I knew there was no way my words would penetrate. My efforts to point out that nothing good would come of the lifestyle he was leading only made him more angry. "Who the fuck are you to tell me what to do?" he'd say. "You aren't my parent. It's not like you even remembered I existed until now. You can't come back after all this time and expect to jump right in and be my brother again."

"Buddy, these guys you're hanging with are bad news," I warned.

"My name is Alex," he'd say. "I ain't your buddy."

Other times he'd throw it in my face that I'd been way worse than him at his age and laugh it off. The laugh was bitter, leaving a chill around my heart.

"And look at what happened to me," I'd say. "My wife left me. I nearly lost my kids. Everything that mattered to me disappeared. And I wasted almost eight years of my life throwing it all away. You want that to happen to you?"

"Fuck you."

After a while, I gave up trying to reach him. It seemed it only ever made him act out more. One night he was out driving around in a rough neighborhood with a couple of his gang member friends trying to buy a dime bag of weed. None of them were aware that blood had been shed between two rival gangs in that area a month before. Guns were fired in a drive-by. That sort of bad business.

When the black kids on the corner saw the unfamiliar van my brother was in cruise down their block that dark night—driven by a young Mexican male—they thought the vehicle was full of rival gang members rolling up on them.

They opened fire.

The driver, my brother's friend Flaco, was shot in the spine.

Another bullet grazed my brother across the abdomen. A second one hit his groin, cutting through his femoral artery.

The other two passengers with them ducked in the backseat of the vehicle, escaping injury.

Seriously wounded himself, Flaco managed to drive to the hospital. The two in the backseat jumped out of the car and fled.

Flaco didn't make it in time. My brother—my Buddy—was pronounced dead on arrival. He was a month shy of his twenty-first birthday.

What followed—the arrest, arraignment, trial, and the ultimate acquittal of the person who allegedly murdered my brother—is perhaps another book, one I'm not yet ready to write. The guilt over how the actions of my misspent youth may have ultimately led my brother to his end is still too overwhelming.

I felt then, as I do now, that I am to blame. I wish I'd been more involved in his life, more supportive and insistent he stay away from gangs and violence, more of a role model. He'd been following in my footsteps, and I had led him straight to the cemetery.

But more than that, I also felt that somehow his death was some sort of divine retribution for all the violence and hate I'd projected into the world, for the pain I'd inflicted on others because of the color of their skin, and my misplaced idea that by hurting them, I could save myself.

My brother was killed because he was in a car with people whose skin color threatened a bunch of scared, ignorant kids with a different skin color.

At the funeral, old skinhead acquaintances of mine, my brother's friends, even family members who I'd never heard utter a racist word in their lives, came up to me to see if I was going to seek revenge. They urged me to. Hungered for it, even. The score had to be settled.

To say I was dumbfounded is an understatement. Full of guilt and regret, the last thing I wanted was to keep the cycle of violence going.

It had to stop with me—with Buddy. I would never again be part of that world of hate.

My brother had died for my sins.

I would spend the rest of my life atoning for them, and it would never bring him back.

EPILOGUE

Over a decade later, I am still trying to recover from the shock of my brother's loss however I can.

While I was earning my bachelor's degree from DePaul University, I had an extraordinary opportunity to work as a rapporteur for the United Nations' 57th Annual Conference on Civil Society and the Millennium Development Goals. As a result, I was able to produce an informational short film, hoping to inspire people to come together in peace to work on serious global issues like poverty, hunger, and HIV/AIDS, and to promote gender parity in developing countries. As my final assignment before graduation, I wrote a twenty-page thesis detailing my involvement in the white supremacist movement and my ultimate disengagement from violent, far-right-wing extremism. Twelve years later, that project became this book.

In 2008, I was invited to write an opinion editorial for the popular music magazine *Alternative Press*, where I denounced my eight years of hate. The publication of that piece was pivotal for me, as it was the first time I'd openly spoken about my past in a large public forum. I urged readers to heed my story and find ways to make the world a better place, a world that promoted inclusion and equality for everyone.

For nearly a decade, I volunteered as a coach for my sons' soccer teams

Christian Picciolini with his sons, Devin and Brandon, Grand Canyon, 2011

and encouraged all the diverse young athletes I mentored to strive for integrity in what they do, both on and off the field.

On Dr. Martin Luther King Jr.'s birthday in 2009, I co-founded Life After Hate, a nonprofit organization that strives to be an agent of change for those struggling with hate. I've also launched a successful intervention assistance program focused on helping people safely leave hate and violence behind. By sharing my unique perspectives on empathy and compassion, and by promoting basic human goodness, I now aspire to be a shining beacon of hope for those who feel mired in racism and prejudice. While regrets over my past still haunt me and I will forever remain reeling from the loss of my brother, I have made meaningful changes in my life and can look in the mirror for the first time in my memory without seeing a monster staring back at me.

I graduated from college and married Britton, the most understanding and loving woman on the planet, someone who has never known a hateful moment. Every day, I thank the gods of fate and destiny for letting my path join with that of a woman of her strength, character, intelligence, empathy, and loving nature.

I have sought to become the father to my sons that I always wished to be. Now that they are young adults, wiser than I ever was at their age, I still hold them accountable for their actions. I am unafraid to talk to them when they do something I know could harm them or someone else. Since taking those first steps away from the movement and toward my children all those years ago, each successive stride became easier. One of the first steps I took, in 1996, during what were some of the darkest days of my depression and fear after I'd left the movement, was to revert to the only thing I knew how to do well—perform music. I put together a little-known punk band called Random55 to try to keep my mind from shutting down. This time the lyrics were about my own pain and loss, not about promoting violence and hatred. I was fortunate enough during my time with Random55 to meet one of the heroes of my youth—the venerated Joan Jett.

An acquaintance I'd met through my record store the previous year was a concert promoter at a club across town. She called me one afternoon when she had a last-minute cancellation from one of the bands she'd booked to open for a major headliner that night. She asked if we could help her out and fill the slot. We were thrilled. Before I could ask who the band was that we'd be supporting, she hung up. We packed our gear and booked it to the club. When we arrived at the venue, we were ecstatic to learn that Random55 would be the opening act for Joan Jett and the Blackhearts.

Shrouded by the excitement of the night, inside I was still battling a solitary depression that all but incapacitated me and constantly made me question whether my life was worth living. Shortly before the doors of the venue opened that evening, as Joan wrapped up her sound check before heading to her dressing room, she noticed me sitting quietly backstage. She must have sensed that I was hurting, because she approached and put her arm around me.

"I saw your sound check earlier," she said. "You guys are good."

"Thank you," I replied. Suddenly becoming starstruck snapped me out of my funk.

"I bet I'll be seeing more of you. What's your name?"

I told her I was Christian, though I think she could have meant my band's name and been too polite to correct me.

"Christian, I'm Joan." I laughed as we shook hands. Of course I knew her name. She put her arm around my shoulder again. "Get up there and warm up the crowd for me." I told her I would.

Backstage later that night, after her second encore, I mentioned to Joan that I had actually met her briefly once before when I was thirteen years old. It had been while she was filming the movie *Light of Day* with Michael J. Fox, which they'd shot partly in Blue Island.

"Thanks for making me feel old," she joked. She started walking away, then stopped and turned around. "Why were you so sad earlier? You guys played a great show to a sold-out crowd. You should be happy."

I told her that I'd been going through a rough patch. "You know, relationships, work, that kind of stuff."

"Well, things will only get better if you let them." Her voice was kind and caring. "We've actually got a tour coming up in the winter. If you guys aren't busy, I'd love it if you and the band would come along and be our support act for a few of those shows."

To this day, those gigs remain some of the highlights of my life. And throughout that short tour, Joan continued to shower me with empathy.

Her words and actions helped save my life. During those dark and confusing days, when I often contemplated whether it was worth living, it was her kindness that lifted my spirits.

All human beings have a need for compassion and possess the ability to give it, but she taught me that empathy—putting yourself in someone else's shoes to allow yourself to understand the pain they are feeling—is the most important thing we can do.

She taught me that we are part of each other. We are bound together by the fact that we are human beings. What becomes of the human race is everyone's responsibility, and when one of us fails, we all do. When one of us refuses to be part of what is wrong with the world, the world becomes brighter for all of us.

She taught me to recognize that and to honor it in my actions and decisions.

She taught me to be part of the good in the world, part of the ever-growing community that seeks fairness, justice, and compassion; that we all have the ability to *make good happen* if we just try.

That you are me, and I am you.

Peace to us all.

STORAGE
BOX
BE
KIND

ACKNOWLEDGMENTS

THIS BOOK WOULD NOT HAVE been possible without the extraordinary support of a number of people, beginning with my incredible wife, Britton, the rock on which my new life has been built. Although I began to take my first few steps toward my transformation before I met you, Britton, you've been the support I have needed to continue to move forward every day. Your wisdom and rational mind are a much-appreciated ballast to my frequent risk-taking and impulsive decisions. You are my partner and best friend, and I am forever grateful for being a part of your life. I can only hope my endless love for you offers some consolation for my numerous preoccupations.

I can't say enough to acknowledge my sons, Devin and Brandon, the catalysts for my awakening. Words cannot express how immensely proud I am of these fine young men. May they remember that all people are imperfect, and that through our imperfections we become part of the same family—the human race. If I could impart any wisdom to them, it is this: follow your dreams, and let your words and actions reflect your true heart. It's ok to be vulnerable, and make sure everything you do benefits peace and promotes acceptance, caring, and equality for everyone. I love you both so much.

Random street art, Chicago (artist unknown)

I want to express my love and gratitude to my parents, Anna and Enzo Picciolini. I owe them both so much for refusing to turn me away when I needed their help the most. Looking back, I fully recognize that they sacrificed their time with me because they loved me and wanted to make a better life for me and Alex than they'd had, and I respect them for that. I thank them for doing their best and for being good and decent people who truly care and love with all their hearts.

Thanks to Zia Lina, to whom I owe all my creative and artistic ambitions. To Zia Mary, whom I miss dearly, whose arms I remember being held in as a small child and whose melodies sang me to sleep. She was the friend I needed growing up. I owe my sense of adventure, my street savvy, and inventiveness to Zio Nando. To you I say, sometimes it takes a bunch of wrong turns in life to eventually stumble back on the right path. These three were my real heroes when I was growing up, and I owe much of my inspiration to them. I hope they continue to influence those around them with their positive presence and caring natures.

I owe a great deal to my indelible memories of Nonno Michele, the grandfather I so admired as an impressionable child. He not only built tables and chairs but also helped build me. And where would I be without Nonna Nancy, who will forever remain in our hearts as the foundation of our family. I miss her toughness, her delicious meatballs, and her constant concern for my untied shoelaces.

My old friend Mike W., who passed too early in life to fully complete his own transformation, showed me that actions truly speak louder than words, even if the actions are those of two misguided, troublemaking kids. He taught me through his unselfish friendship that loyalty and support for family and loved ones are things you uphold first and ask questions about later. From him I learned that having someone you can trust and rely on makes you strive to become a better person yourself, so you can become someone they can trust and rely on when they need you.

To Sarge, my old friend, it was me who drank all your beer that night. I hope you are finally free. Rest in peace, fella.

Peace, love, and gratitude go to my extended Formers family—some of the most remarkable and transformed human beings on this planet. Thank you for your continued human resilience, your critical insights, and your daily inspiration. Live and love.

Mr. Johnny Holmes, thank you for helping me realize I needed to forgive myself before I could seek forgiveness from others. Your kindness kept me alive and gave me hope when I wasn't sure who I was or how to move forward.

Joan Jett, what can I say? You are as awe-inspiring to me today as the first day I heard your voice and music all those years ago. What you said to me in 1996, my old friend, struck a chord, and I have never forgotten it. You are an amazing woman and an inspiring human being. On behalf of all those you've touched and stood shoulder to shoulder with over the decades: thank you.

Many thanks to my dear friend (and former ideological foe) Nora Flanagan, the coolest and most tattooed English teacher I know. If not for her friendship and invariable nudging, this book might never have been completed.

To my friend Michael Mohr, I'm so grateful we embarked on this journey together. Your invaluable insight and constant encouragement every time I threw my exhausted hands up pushed me to become a better writer and a better person. You also taught me to "kill my darlings" and, in the process, made me love the art of writing. Thank you.

I also want to send a big thanks to the team at Hachette Books—especially my editors Mauro DiPreta and David Lamb—and to my agents, Mark Falkin, Michael Smallbone, and Sean Berard, for always believing in me and this project. And to my lovely and tough-as-nails assistant, Shannon Martinez, thank you for being my backup hard drive, extra battery, cheerleader, and friend.

To all those supporters and friends who constantly encourage me to keep fighting the good fight, I could not have done this without you. Thank you so very much.

And lastly in mention but always first in my heart, this book is for Alex. My brother. My Buddy. The greatest regret in my life is not being there for you when you needed me. You inspired me to write about my story, and your tragic loss showed me that life is something to be respected, cherished, and remembered, never taken for granted or forgotten—no matter how dark some of the memories might be. We have not been the same since you left us.

ABOUT THE AUTHOR

CHRISTIAN PICCIOLINI IS AN EMMY AWARD–winning television producer, a visual artist, a renowned public speaker, and a reformed extremist. His work and life purpose are born of an ongoing and profound need to atone for a grisly past, and to make something of his time on this planet by contributing to the greater good.

After leaving the violent hate movement he was part of during his youth, he began the painstaking process of rebuilding his life. While working for IBM, Picciolini earned a degree from DePaul University and later began his own global entertainment media firm. He has worked as an adjunct professor at the college level, and as the community partnerships manager for Threadless.

In 2009 he co-founded Life After Hate, a nonprofit dedicated to helping others combat hate. He is tirelessly committed to helping individuals around the world disengage from all forms of racism and violent extremism.

An explorer by nature, Picciolini loves to learn new things and thrives on challenging himself with "positive disruptive thinking." He values kindness, sincerity, and respect for all people, and believes that small ideas and a little compassion can change the world.

Christian Picciolini (Photo by Dennis Sevilla)